Happiness to the power of infinity

By

Rohit Sodha

ISBN 9781093260212

Credits for cover design: Sandeep Singh and team
Credits for images: Licensed images from Pexel

Dedicated to Papai, Papa-Hukum, Amma and Dadisa

"You continue to guide us – from heaven"

"Happiness is to life what fizz is
to soda"
Rohit Sodha

Table of contents

Author's note

Why a book on happiness?

"Life is better when you are happy" – Rohit Sodha

Why do we do all the things that we do in life? Making friends, falling in love, marrying, having kids, building a career, studying, exercising, eating healthy, practicing spirituality, travelling – we do this to achieve a particular goal, the achievement of which is knowingly or unknowingly linked to us making ourselves happy. We focus so much on the intermediate goal that often we neglect how important and omnipresent the overarching end goal is – HAPPINESS. It is central to our existence – the soul of our lives. Everything we do is with the inherent intention of making us happy – largely without us even being aware about it.

Despite happiness being so central to our lives there is little that we actively do about it. We cant and don't really measure it, we don't clearly know what triggers happiness and what does not, and we don't actively work to improve it. Compare this with physical fitness – a multibillion dollar industry exists around it guiding us on how to become and stay healthy. We know our starting point: body weight, BMI, muscle percentage, current eating habits etc and we set a target – particular weight with a particular BMI and a muscle percentage. There is a stringent path to the target state – involving highly regimented exercise schedule and dietary choices to be made over weeks if not months. How to get from initial to final stage is shared with us through all kinds of media – books, apps, internet videos, DVDs, gyms, personal trainers, nutritionists, chefs and all the rigmarole that you can imagine.

This is why I decided to write a book on happiness – to make it tangible for you, to make it personal for your individual personality and finally to have it as your guide through life for becoming and staying happy. Actually let me rephrase myself, this is not a book – this is a self-help guide which you should work with to make yourself happier and stay that way throughout life.

The obvious next question is – how will this self help guide help me do what it is promising to do: Ive developed a patented 3 step system called HappSys to becoming happy and staying happy – 1. LifeJourney 2. HappFrame and 3. HappIndex. We will work together through this guide on these core building blocks of a happiness system that is built for your specific needs and that adjusts with your changing priorities in life as you progress with life. More on these three elements in a bit.

This guide will help you bring positive change to your life without you having to make any major changes – sounds crazy doesn't it! I will show you how you can achieve incremental happiness by tweaking minor behaviors and dealing with emotional impulses better to accentuate their positive impact and limiting the harm they may cause. This is not a guide that preaches – it helps you take charge and drive desired outcomes by making minor tweaks to how you go about living your life.

Who am I to write a book on happiness?

I'm not a doctor, nurse, psychologist, spiritual guru, life coach, religious leader, fitness instructor, counsellor, economist, political leader or researcher and I have also not had any transformational life experiences like near death events, tremendous emotional upheaval or disproportionate misery caused by socioeconomic or other factors which have suddenly unlocked profound wisdom which no other human being had access to before me. I am a common man like millions of you – living a common life – married, 2 kids and working in a corporate job. And like millions of you disillusioned by the concept of happiness and trying to be happy while going about our lives I also didn't find any self help guide which could help me become happier. Therefore, I started researching this topic – read dozens of books, thousands of articles and finally developed a system that is generic in its concept but unique in its applicability. Like the founder of Porsche said – "I couldn't find the sports car of my dreams, so I built it myself." I am on a similar mission – be happier myself and build a system which everyone can adopt and become happy. This endeavor culminated with HappSys – a globally applicable individually customizable happiness system. HappSys can be practiced by every human being on planet earth and will help each one of you become happier and make our beautiful planet an even happier place!

Who is this book for?

I will commit marketing hara-kiri by not identifying a 'target audience' for my self-help guide. This powerful tool is for people who want to be high achievers – anyone who aspires to be good at something – a good leader, a good employee, a good father, a good student, a good mother, a good sister, a good teacher, a good son, a good sportsperson.

This book is for the young and old, healthy and sick, rich and poor, powerful and powerless, winners, losers, hopefuls – this guide doesn't discriminate or judge on the basis of race, religion, sexual orientation, disability, nationality, skin color, spiritual beliefs, language or anything else – happiness is as common and natural to mankind as red being the color of blood irrespective of all what differentiates us. Whether you are a multibillionaire tech mogul or struggling to make ends meet this guide has something for you; whether you are from the US, Canada, Brazil, Mexico, Germany, France, Sweden, Norway, Nigeria, Sudan, Dubai, China, Japan, India, Bangladesh or Australia there is something in this guide for you; whether you are studying to get a degree and enter the job market or preparing to retire there is something for you – you get it – no matter who you are this guide has something for you.

What this book is not?

This is not a doctor's prescription, this is not a psychiatrist explaining chemicals that will drive happiness, this is not a yoga lesson, this is not 'give away all your material belongings and become an ascetic' sermon, this is not a relationship counselling session, this is not spiritual guidance, this is not dietary guidance, this is not fitness advice – In summary this is not professional advice on one or more specific areas that you may need support on in your life. This is also not preachy – I will not tell you to do something because I think it will make you happy. I will be your partner in helping you discover yourself, discover what drives happiness in your life and how to enhance your happiness by making small practical tweaks.

Think of it as a painting session where I help you find your inner painter and provide you with the direction to enable you to create your own masterpiece – something that you and your loved ones will value. And if you are not a painter we will together find something else that you enjoy doing. It doesn't matter if the world values it or not – it is your prized memory – just like the first words that your baby may have spoken, just like the first time you fell in love, just like the breath of fresh air coming from the sea.

Happiness to the power of infinity

Happiness

a. What is happiness?

The Oxford dictionary describes 'Happiness' as a noun which means 'the state of being happy'. That doesn't explain much. So, what does it mean to be happy and where does this word originally come from? The word happiness is at the confluence of philosophy and psychology. In philosophy, happiness has its origins from the Greek concept of 'Eudaimonia' – Aristotle, Socrates, Plato, Epicurus and others have mentioned what it is that human beings need to achieve the state of eudaimonia – a mix of moral virtues and actions. Surprisingly worldly achievements have been left out. This is unimaginable in the world where we live in – it is well known that the happiest countries in the world according to the 'World Happiness report 2018' published by the United Nations there is a strong correlation between GDP per capita (or in simple terms wealth of people) and happiness. The top 10 ranked countries are all countries with high GDP per capita and disposable incomes; conversely the lowest ranked countries are all with low income levels. We will talk about this in more detail later.

In psychology, happiness is a mental or emotional state of well-being which can be defined by, among others, positive or pleasant emotions ranging from contentment to intense joy. There are two components to happiness – 1. Feelings of happiness and 2. Thoughts of satisfaction with life. In scientific literature, 'feelings of happiness' is referred to as hedonia (Ryan & Deci, 2001), the presence of positive emotions and the absence of negative emotions. Pleasure, comfort, gratitude, hope, and inspiration are examples of positive emotions that increase our happiness. Feelings of happiness are momentary in nature and can be invoked by targeted action in the short term like eating an ice-cream, catching up with a friend, listening to music or going for a nature walk. Hedonia is also about having negative emotions infrequently – emotions of fear, distress, shame, guilt, irritability, hostility, nervousness, anger and other negative feelings. This makes the overall concept of happiness more actionable – we can tune our mind and body to believe we are happy atleast for the moment. This is a big lever that we have in our hands to drive happiness sporadically. It is true that human life cannot be imagined without the absence of negative emotions but through HappSys I will provide to you a tactical system of developing a way to live to avoid situations which trigger these emotions, creating a safety net around you to deflect such emotions and how to actively manage these negative feelings.

"Many of us pursue pleasure with such breathless haste that we hurry past it." Søren Kierkegaard

There is a limit, however, to how much you can momentarily boost your mind to believe you are happy and there is a downside to artificially boosting momentary happiness. Too much icecream without exercise will lead to weight gain and obesity and reduced long term happiness – this is called the paradox of hedonism. There is also a negative side to hedonism – humans if not held back by social or moral principles will indulge in creating happiness for themselves causing harm to themselves and others knowingly or unknowingly. Think of wild drunken parties with reckless sexual behavior that gives happiness for the short term but damages health due to overconsumption of alcohol and creates a longer lasting feeling of guilt for people who are in committed relationships; this also risks lifelong valuable relationships for momentary pleasure.

Without the second element of happiness – 'satisfaction with life', the first element will only act as the emergency wheel when one of the main tyres of your life's car gets punctured and will only get you that far on your journey. Both these elements should be treated as supplementary rather than complementary to each other. Think of it as vitamins and other nutrients for your body. We need it all to have a balanced diet – the exclusion of any of the key elements will lead to disease and deteriorated health condition. What is 'satisfaction with life'? Psychologists call it 'eudaimonia' and in common language it refers to overall how satisfied you are with your life – do you think you are growing as a person in all spheres of life important to you – professionally, financially, spiritually, are you being able to achieve the purpose of your life that you set out to achieve, do you think that life has progressed in the medium to long term in a positive direction for you?

Eudaimonia is often translated as "happiness," but that's a bit misleading. Eudaimonia comes from two Greek words:
Eu-: good
Daimon: soul or "self". A difficult word to translate into English.

Socrates believed that human beings desire the state of eudaimonia more than anything else. However, Socrates believed that virtues such as justice, courage, self-control and wisdom were essential and, when practiced, sufficient to achieve eudaimonia. Virtue, he held, was a form of knowledge of both good and evil that is necessary to achieve the ultimate good (eudaimonia) desired by all human beings.

Aristotle wrote about the idea the most, and it was important to many Greek philosophers, from Socrates, the father of Greek philosophy, through to Stoicism, a late-Greek philosophy. You can achieve Eudaimonia, Aristotle argued, by working hard, cultivating your virtues, and excelling at whatever tasks nature and circumstances come to you. However, Aristotle also wrote that living in the right kind of place and balancing your activities with wisdom are essential to achieving Eudaimonia as well.

"Happiness is the meaning and the purpose of life, the whole aim and end of human existence." Aristotle

"Happiness" is an emotion, whereas Eudaimonia is a much more comprehensive state of being. Happiness is something that a person might create or lose at any moment, while Eudaimonia takes long effort to build and has staying power. Happiness, for some people, can be gotten through simple pleasures, like eating, or by immoral means, like stealing. Whereas Eudaimonia includes being a good person, and doesn't come from pleasure, although, hopefully, it does lead to pleasure.

"The ultimate end of human acts is Eudaimonia, happiness in the sense of living well, which all men desire; all acts are but different means chosen to arrive at it." - Hannah Arendt

The concepts of 'hedonia' and 'eudaimonia' lead us to question how much of happiness is really in our control. Psychologist Sonja Lyubomirsky in her book "The how of happiness" explains the 50-10-40 formula. 50% of your happiness is determined by your genes, 10% by your circumstances and 40% is determined by your actions.

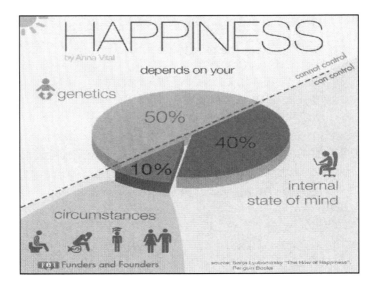

Genetics is the study of heredity. Heredity is a biological process where a parent passes certain genes onto their children or offspring. Every child inherits genes from both of their biological parents and these genes in turn express specific traits. Some of these traits may be physical for example hair and eye color and skin color etc. On the other hand some genes may also carry the risk of certain diseases and disorders that may pass on from parents to their offspring. Our genes are clearly something we inherit and cannot control. You are gifted or cursed as you are born and you can do nothing about it. The good news is that the other two factors are in our control to varying degrees though.

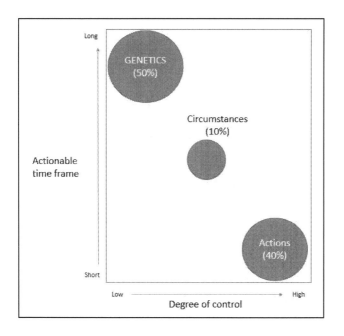

Circumstances are at a lower degree of control as compared to actions. According to multiple studies, life circumstances that influence our happiness level are: personal experiences, occupation, health, income, religious beliefs, marital status, age, gender, geographic factors. Let me give you an example, if you are poor and uneducated and live in a country mired with socio-economic unrest and war, it will take you a lot of effort and time to change the circumstances you live in. You will have to acquire education and consequently or inconsequently wealth, either wait for the conditions in your country to improve or move to a country with better living conditions. While all of this is possible and has been done by hundreds of thousands of people who have moved in the history of mankind to a better place to have a better future – this takes a lot of grit, determination, effort and time to do so. Conversely if you are well educated, live in a secure environment with a good financial status your 'circumstances' are good and consequently your happiness score.

The most actionable and easy to implement factor contributing to 40% of your happiness is clearly within your own hands. Intentional activities which are responsible for 40% of our happiness level mean those cognitive, behavioral and volitional activities which we choose to do. They require effort.

So 50% of your happiness is in your hands and 80% of the 50% is actionable in the short term easily. This is great news! A lot of us don't realize this and remain chronically unhappy. Let us in the course of this book try and find together a sustainable system of happiness which we can all implement in our lives and be happy.

a.   What happens when we are happy?

When we are happy we obviously smile and laugh but there are also a thousand other changes that are happening in the body and the mind. An authentic smile (as opposed to a fake one) can be identified by looking at the eyes of the person smiling – if they get the 'happiness' crow feet

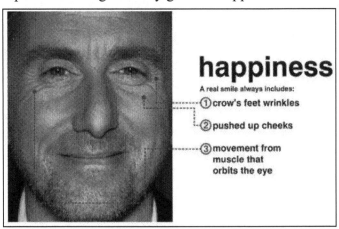

happiness

A real smile always includes:

① crow's feet wrinkles

② pushed up cheeks

③ movement from muscle that orbits the eye

wrinkles, if the cheeks are pushed up and if the muscle orbiting the eye shows movement then the smile is surely a genuine one.

In addition to the obvious smile, our backs straighten up when we are happy and any kind of slouching or kneeling ends; our body opens up and we undo crossed legs, hands etc opening up the body to take in the positivity around us.

There is a lot more going on in the brain that is not so visible as the body. Our brain releases a variety of chemicals when we experience different kinds of emotions.

- Dopamine: the go-getter. Dopamine motivates you to take action and encourages the persistence required to meet your needs, seek reward, or approach a goal – whether it's a sports competition, a commercial negotiation or starting to look for your new job. The anticipation of the reward is actually what triggers a dopamine good feeling in your brain causing it to release the energy you need to move towards the reward. Then, you get another pleasure hit when you successfully meet the need. You can stimulate the good feeling of dopamine by embracing a new goal and breaking it down into achievable steps, rather than only allowing your brain to celebrate when you hit the finish line. The idea is to create a series of small successes which keeps the dopamine flowing in your brain. And it's important to actually celebrate every accomplishment – give yourself gifts commensurate to the achievement

- Oxytocin – the cuddler: Oxytocin is released through closeness with another person and helps to create intimacy and trust and build healthy relationships. Skin-to-skin contact releases oxytocin, for example a person gets a hit during orgasm and mothers do during childbirth and breastfeeding. The cultivation of oxytocin increases fidelity and is essential for creating and maintaining strong bonds and improved social interactions. You can also boost oxytocin in other ways besides cuddling. The release of oxytocin can also be triggered through social bonding, like eye contact and attentiveness. A simple way to get an oxytocin surge is to give someone a hug – even your pet!

- Serotonin – the confidence booster: Serotonin plays many different roles in your brain but mainly it can be thought of as the confidence molecule and flows when you feel significant or important and controls your overall mood. If you're in a good mood, you've got serotonin to thank. You enjoy the good feeling of serotonin when you feel respected by others, and your brain seeks more of that good feeling by repeating the behaviors that triggered it in your past. The respect you got in your youth paved neural pathways that tell your brain how to get respect today.

- Endorphins – the fighter: Endorphins have a chemical structure similar to opiates, mask pain or discomfort, and are associated with the fight or flight response. Endorphins give you the oomph to help you power through any situation. The word endorphin literally means "self-produced morphine," and conversely to what you might think, pain actually causes endorphins to be released. Similar to morphine, they act as an analgesic and sedative, diminishing your perception of pain. You've probably heard of an "endorphin high." Well, a runner doesn't get that feeling unless they push their body to the point of distress. Endorphins helped our ancestors survive in emergencies, for example they could still run away when injured, but if you were on an endorphin high all the time, you would touch a hot stove or walk on a broken leg. Endorphins are produced during strenuous physical exertion, sexual intercourse and orgasm. Laughing and stretching also cause you to release endorphins because both of these agitate your insides, causing moderate wear and tear and moderate endorphin flow.

b.   Benefits of happiness

No matter where you live, what your occupation is, what socio-economic background you have – happiness will bring benefits to you, your family, your coworkers, your community, your country and this world. Being happy has a positive impact on physical and mental health, increases efficiency of the labor force, improves the quality of your relationships, reduces crime and social unrest and even gets people to pay more taxes! Im not kidding!

- Health benefits: There is abundance of research strongly linking happiness to better physical and mental health. Happy people live longer, have lower stress levels and less diseases and aches and pains. Two studies on longevity have been quoted in scientific circles - one conducted in 2011 in England amongst adults aged 52-79 showed happier people were 35% less likely to die in the next 5 years as compared to their less happier participants; Participants were asked to record how happy, excited and content they were multiple times a day.

  The other study was published in 2001 by the American Psychological Association and was conducted on Catholic nuns. Autobiographical essays written by the nuns when they entered the convent decades (typically in their 20s) were studied by researches for positive feelings of gratitude, contentment and joy. The study concluded that the happiest nuns lived 7-10 years longer than the least happy nuns. Happy people are less stressed too – in a study where participants were asked to record their happiness more than 30 times a day the happiest participants had 23% lower levels of stress hormore cortisone than the least happy. Happiness also helps recover from stressful experiences faster – a study in 2009 on psychology students where students were asked whether they generally felt positive feelings after which they were asked to answer a tough statistics question while being videotaped and the answer of which would be evaluated by the professor – the happiest students recovered most quickly. Happy people are also less prone to diseases and aches and pains. In a 2003 experiment 350 adults volunteered to get exposed to common cold – after 5 days in quarantine – the participants with the most positive emotions were the least likely to catch the cold. If governments take into account these factors, imagine how many billions of dollars can be saved – less days in hospital for every patient, less medication, less usage of disposable materials, fewer meals, less laundry etc. These savings can then be ploughed back into the system to provide basic healthcare to the millions of people who do not have access currently.

- Work efficiency: A study by Daniel Sgroy found that happy employees are up to 20% more productive than unhappy employees. In the book, The Happiness Advantage, salespeople were studied and it was found that happiness has an even greater impact - raising sales by 37%, productivity by 31% and accuracy on tasks by 19%. But the benefits don't end there. Happy employees are also good news for organizations: The stock prices of Fortune's "100 Best Companies to Work for" rose 14% per year from 1998 to 2005, while companies not on the list only reported a 6% increase. Most companies have started some sort of an employee engagement program ranging from organizing office events to free meals, massages, childcare services on campus etc but very few have truly understood what it takes to keep their workforce happy, satisfied and motivated and even fewer have been able to develop effective programs to be able to do that on a sustainable basis. If you are a business leader, imagine the great benefits you can bring to your organization by keeping your employees happy. There is a ton of research out there on this topic

- Relationships: Your relationships can have a large impact on your sense of well-being, and your actions and moods can influence the people with whom you come in contact. There's also evidence that when you become happier, it helps those around you increase their own happiness. Results from the large Framingham Heart Study showed that when people became happy, their nearby friends experienced a 25% greater chance of becoming happy, and their next-door neighbors had a 34% increase. In their report in an issue of British Medical Journal, researchers from the University of California, San Diego, and Harvard Medical School concluded that "people's happiness depends on the happiness of others with whom they are connected." So working toward your own happiness can benefit the people around you as well. As we can see it is clearly a team sport. We are discussing improved quality of relationships as a result of happiness but it is also a key driver of happiness. Later in the book we will discuss how to build healthy, mutually beneficial relationships and actively manage toxic relations

- Lower crime and substance abuse: In a study conducted by the University of California in 2011, it was concluded that happier adolescents were less likely to report involvement in crime or drug use. Adolescents with minor, or nonclinical, depression had significantly higher odds of engaging in such activities. The study also found that changes in emotions over time matter. Adolescents who experienced a decrease in their level of happiness or an increase in the degree of their depression over a one-year period had higher odds of being involved in crime and of using drugs. Most adolescents experience both happiness and depression, and the study finds that the relative intensity of these emotions is also important. The odds of drug use were notably lower for youth who reported that they were more often happy than depressed, and were substantially higher for those who indicated that they were more depressed than happy

- Happier nations collect more taxes! Norway Denmark and Iceland have consistently been at the top of the rankings of the happiest countries in the world by the UN for the last 3 years. These countries are also amongst the highest taxed in the OECD group of countries. The widely enjoyed social benefits residents get in exchange for their taxes, such as universal health care, access to education and subsidized parental leave, create "strong social foundations" and a feeling of mutual trust between the state and its citizens. This further increases the citizens' willingness to pay higher taxes and the state symbiotically being able to invest further in improvement of its services towards its citizens.

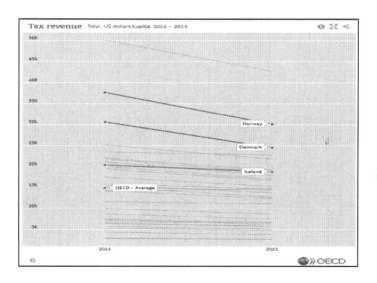

"The foolish man seeks happiness in the distance, the wise grows it under his feet"

James Oppenheim

c.   Why is happiness at the core of life?

Imagine your life where you have all that you have always desired to have – you have achieved all goals set for yourself – there is nothing that you wanted that you have not been able to get. What would this do to you? How would you feel? It is probably accurate to say you would atleast feel happy.

Happiness is therefore the outcome of us being able to achieve what we strive for and work hard towards.

Major religions of the world preach happiness as a central theme of life and I will talk about each one of them in some detail. I would like to point out that the system I have developed blends relevant teachings from all major religions, adapts it to practical modern lives and makes it actionable on a daily basis for you. But first let us learn about how various religions preach happiness.

Buddhism: Buddhism is a religion to about 300 million people around the world. The word comes from 'budhi' which in ancient Sanskrit language means 'to awaken'. It has its origins about 2,500 years ago when Siddhartha Gautama a prince born into a royal family in ancient India, now known as the Buddha, was himself awakened (enlightened) at the age of 35. At 29, he realised that wealth and luxury did not guarantee happiness, so he explored the different teachings religions and philosophies of the day, to find the key to human happiness. After six years of study and meditation he finally found 'the middle path' and was enlightened. After enlightenment, the Buddha spent the rest of his life teaching the principles of Buddhism — called the Dhamma, or Truth — until his death at the age of 80. The Buddha taught many things, but the basic concepts in

Buddhism can be summed up by the Four Noble Truths and the Noble Eightfold Path.

The Four Noble Truths are:

- The Truth of Suffering: After his experiences as a prince and as a wandering monk, the Buddha had learnt that all people have one thing in common: if they think about their own life, or look at the world around them, they will see that life is full of suffering. Suffering, he said, may be physical or mental. The Buddha's most important teachings were focused on a way to end the suffering he had experienced and had seen in other people. His discovery of the solution began with the recognition that life is suffering. Suffering is a fact of life. There are four unavoidable physical sufferings; birth, old age, sickness and death. There are also three forms of mental suffering; separation from the people we love; contact with people we dislike and frustration of desires. Happiness is real and comes in many ways, but happiness does not last forever and does not stop suffering. Buddhists believe that the way to end suffering is to first accept the fact that suffering is actually a fact of life.

- The Truth of the Cause of Suffering: After the Buddha learnt that suffering is a part of life, he realised he could not find a way to end suffering without finding out what causes it. Buddhists study that the Buddha learnt this just like a doctor learns about what's wrong with his patient by listing their symptoms, finding out what makes them worse and studying other cases before prescribing a cure. By watching people Buddha found out that the causes of suffering are craving and desire, and ignorance. The power of these things to cause all suffering is what Buddhists call The Second Noble Truth. Craving can be explained as the strong desires that people have for pleasing their senses and for experiencing life itself. Buddhists believe that anything that stimulates our senses or our feelings can lead to craving. People everywhere crave for their favourite tastes, but we all know that not even the best sweets and our favourite meal lasts forever. Soon it is finished and there can be no more to enjoy, and then it is forgotten as though it never even happened. None of the pleasures we crave for ever give us lasting happiness or satisfaction. This is why people can crave to repeat these experiences again and again, and become unhappy and dissatisfied until they can satisfy their craving. What is ignorance? Real ignorance is not just being uneducated, or not knowing many things. Buddhists see ignorance as the inability to see the truth about things, to see things as they really are. This ability to see the truth is not a question of either eyesight or education. Buddhists believe that there are many truths about the world that people are ignorant of, because of the limits of their understanding.

- The Truth of the End of Suffering: After the Buddha realised the Truth about suffering and its causes, he spent six years committed to discovering a realization about the end of suffering — that, and his achievement of Nirvana, were his ultimate achievements. In those six years, the Buddha tried all the methods available to end suffering without success. Eventually He found his own solution to the problems of life and they are now the core of Buddhist thought, teachings and practice. This is what he discovered: there is an end to suffering; it can happen to anybody, anywhere, here and now; and the key to ending all suffering is to remove all desire, ill will and ignorance. After suffering, the Buddha taught, there is supreme happiness. Every step of the way to removing the causes of unhappiness brings more joy. On the path to the end of suffering, which is a path that Buddhists may spend their whole lifetimes practicing, there are levels of happiness and freedom from craving and ignorance that can be achieved. In the beginning the happiness might be through better material conditions: like more contentment, or better spiritual conditions; more peace and enjoyment of life. These are the reasons Buddhists can live happily without greed — even among people in cities overcome with craving and desire. They can live happily without anger even among people harbouring ill will. These kinds of happiness make life more rewarding and bring a sense of freedom and joy. The Buddhist teachings say that the more people free themselves from desire, ill will and ignorance, the greater their happiness is — no matter what is going on around them. When they have completely removed desire, ill will and ignorance the Buddha says they will experience the same supreme happiness he discovered

- The Truth of the Path leading to the End of Suffering: In the beginning, Prince Siddhartha lived in luxury and wealth in his father's palace. After he renounced his privileged life and became a wandering monk, he experienced the hardship and difficulty of a life with nothing. He spent years torturing his mind with hard thoughts and solitude and starved his body, enjoyed no comforts and suffered all the experiences of a life without belongings. Not long before he achieved his insights and attained enlightenment, he realised both these extreme ways of life were as fruitless as each other. He realised that the true way to happiness was to avoid these extremes, to follow a moderate a way of life. He called this way of living the Middle Path. Buddhists describe the three ways of life by comparing them to strings of a lute. The loose string is like a life of careless indulgence and makes a poor note when played. The tight string is like a life of extreme hardship and denial, producing another bad sound when played and, worse, likely to snap at any moment. Only the middle string, which is neither slack nor tense, produces a harmonious note — it has the same qualities as the Middle Path. Those who follow this way, avoid the extremes of indulgence and denial. They do not seek endless pleasures, and they do not torment themselves with pain, lacking and self-torment. The Fourth Noble Truth is that the Middle Path leads to the end of suffering.

The Noble Eightfold Path

The eightfold path, although referred to as steps on a path, is not meant as a sequential learning process, but as eight aspects of life, all of which are to be integrated in every day life. Thus the environment is created to move closer to the Buddhist path. The eightfold path is at the heart of the middle way, which turns from extremes, and encourages us to seek the simple approach. The eightfold path is Right Understanding, Right Intent, Right Speech, Right Action, Right Livelihood, Right Effort, Right Mindfulness, and Right Concentration.

In Buddhism, the eightfold path is meant as a guideline, to be considered, to be contemplated, and to be taken on when, and only when each step is fully accepted as part of the life you seek. Buddhism never asks for blind faith, it seeks to promote learning and a process of self-discovery. The meaning of Right has several aspects, and includes an ethical, and a balanced, or middle way. When things go "right", we often experience a special feeling inside which confirms that this is the correct decision or action.

Right Understanding:

The first step of the eightfold path is Right Understanding or Right View.

This is a significant step on the path as it relates to seeing the world and everything in it as it really is, not as we believe it to be or want it to be. Just as you may read the directions on a map, and then make the journey, studying, reading and examining the information is important, but only the preparation for the journey. At a deeper level, direct personal experience will then lead us to Right Understanding.

In his book " Old Path, White Clouds" , Thich Nhat Hanh tells the story of the Buddha. The Buddha says "my teaching is not a dogma or a doctrine, but no doubt some people will take it as such." The Buddha goes on to say "I must state clearly that my teaching is a method to experience reality and not reality itself, just as a finger pointing at the moon is not the moon itself. A thinking person makes use of the finger to see the moon. A person who only looks at the finger and mistakes it for the moon will never see the real moon." Knowing reality is of very little value if we don't put it to personal use in our lives.

Right Intent:

The second step on the Eightfold Path is Right Intent. This is the step where we become committed to the path. Right Understanding shows us what life really is and what life's problems are composed of, Right Intent urges us to decide what our heart wants. Right Intent must come from the heart and involves recognising the equality of all life and compassion for all that life, beginning with yourself. Right Intent means persistence and a passion for the journey. Setting out to climb a high mountain means you must understand the lay of the land and the pitfalls, the other team members, and the equipment you need. This is similar to Right Understanding. But you will only climb the mountain if you really want to and have a passion for the climb. This is Right Intent. The mountain we climb here is our journey though life. To summarise, Right Understanding will eliminate ignorance. With Right Intent and correct understanding, we then remove desire, which in turn causes the suffering defined in the Four Noble Truths.

Right Speech:

Right Speech is the next step of the Path. We tend to underestimate the power of the spoken word, and often regret words said in haste. Each of us has experienced the disappointment associated with harsh criticism, whether justified or not, and we also are likely to have felt good when kind words encouraged us.

Right speech involves recognition of the truth, and also an awareness of the impact of idle gossip and of repeating rumours. Communicating thoughtfully helps to unite others, and can heal dissention. By resolving never to speak unkindly, or in anger, a spirit of consideration evolves which moves us closer to everyday compassionate living.

Right Action:

Right Action recognises the need to take the ethical approach in life, to consider others and the world we live in. This includes not taking what is not given to us, and having respect for the agreements we make both in our private and business lives. Right Action also encompasses the five precepts which were given by the Buddha, not to kill, steal, lie, to avoid sexual misconduct, and not to take drugs or other intoxicants. This step on the path also includes a whole approach to the environment, with Right Action being taken whenever possible to safeguard the world for future generations.

Right Livelihood:

The next on the Eightfold Path follows on from Right Action, and this is Right Livelihood. If your work has a lack of respect for life, then it will be a barrier to progress on the spiritual path. Buddhism promotes the principle of equality of all living beings and respect for all life.

Certain types of work were discouraged by the Buddha, in particular those where you deal in harmful drugs and intoxicants, those dealing in weapons, and those harmful to animal or human life. So a dedicated Buddhist would not be recommended to have a liquor store, own a gun shop, or be a butcher. In his time, he also discouraged the slave trade, which dealt in human workers. And he was also against the practice of fortune telling as this made assumptions about a fixed future, where his teaching stresses that the future is created by what we do today. Right Livelihood also implies that a Buddhist who is able, will undertake some work, either as part of a Buddhist community, or in the workplace, or, alternatively, do home based or community service. Many communities of monks ensure that each member has daily chores, which remind him of this step on the Eightfold Path.

Right Effort:

Right Effort means cultivating an enthusiasm, a positive attitude in a balanced way. Like the strings of a musical instrument, the amount of effort should not be too tense or too impatient, as well as not too slack or too laid back. Right Effort should produce an attitude of steady and cheerful determination. In order to produce Right Effort, clear and honest thoughts should be welcomed, and feelings of jealousy and anger left behind. Right Effort equates to positive thinking, followed by focused action.

Right Mindfulness:

While Right Effort is a very easy concept for most of us, Right Mindfulness is somewhat trickier to grasp, and may involve quite a change of thinking. Right Mindfulness means being aware of the moment, and being focused in that moment. When we travel somewhere, we are hearing noises, seeing buildings, trees, advertising, feeling the movement, thinking of those we left behind, thinking of our destination. So it is with most moments of our lives.

Right Mindfulness asks us to be aware of the journey at that moment, and to be clear and undistracted at that moment. Right Mindfulness is closely linked with meditation and forms the basis of meditation.

Right Mindfulness is not an attempt to exclude the world, in fact, the opposite. Right Mindfulness asks us to be aware of the moment, and of our actions at that moment. By being aware, we are able to see how old patterns and habits control us. In this awareness, we may see how fears of possible futures limit our present actions. Sometimes you may be absorbed in what you are doing. Music, art, sport can trigger these moments. Have you ever done anything where your mind is only with that activity? At that moment, you are mindful, and the Buddha showed how to integrate that awareness into our everyday lives.

Right Concentration:

Once the mind is uncluttered, it may then be concentrated to achieve whatever is desired. Right Concentration is turning the mind to focus on an object, such as a flower, or a lit candle, or a concept such as loving compassion. This forms the next part of the meditation process. Right concentration implies that we select worthy directions for the concentration of the mind, although everything in nature, beautiful and ugly, may be useful for concentration. At deeper levels, no object or concept may be necessary for further development.

The benefits of Right Mindfulness and Right Concentration are significant as they teach the mind to see things, not as we are conditioned to seeing them, but as they really are. At the same time, they also lead to a feeling of calm and peace with the world. By being in the moment and being able to concentrate effectively, a sense of joy in the moment is felt. Release from the control of past pains and future mind games takes us closer to freedom from suffering.

Hinduism

Happiness and well being is at the core of Hinduism – arguably the oldest religion in the world practiced by more than a billion people today. Happiness has three aspects in Hinduism:

- Physical: also refered to as 'Bhautika' or 'Sukham' in Sanskrit language refers to pleasures which can be felt by the physical body. This includes creature comforts, sensual pleasure and other forms of pleasure which our body can feel directly. This is a very practical aspect of the Hindu religion which acknowledges that human beings need physical pleasures experienced directly by the body. This can have many manifestations ranging from good sex to reduction in physical labour to having the means which make our day to day lives easier. This is the most quantifiable and easily recognizable form of happiness for all of us. We all strive for wordly things in life – good source of income, comfortable homes, good conjugal relations with our partner, financial security and the like. We do this so that our lives and those of our dependents or loved ones are comfortable.

- Mental: also called 'Manasika' or 'Anandam' in Sanskrit language arises from a sense of fulfilment and freedom from anxiety and worries. Being thankful for, being content with and appreciating what you have will lead to mental happiness. Many of us do not fully value what we have and only realize the true value when it is lost. Do you adequately value what you have - Do you value your health? Your family – grandparents, parents, siblings, spouse, children, uncles and aunts? Your close friends? Your job? The place where you were raised and where you live? Do you value the small things that give you pleasure? Four seasons? Natural beauty around you? We always tend to take what we have for granted and strive for the next level of attainment. Most of us in corporate jobs will always try to get promoted, earn more, have a bigger house, fancier car etc. It is normal and healthy to strive for and work towards achieving more but losing mental peace over this is surely not leading to happiness. Another way of looking at it can be doing what is supposed to be done diligently to achieve a goal and not worrying about the outcome. When we directly link our efforts being put in to the achievement of a goal it can sometimes lead to frustration if the achievement of the goal is delayed or cannot be achieved.

- Spiritual: also called 'Adhyaatmika' or 'Paramananda' in Sanskrit refers to the ultimate union with self, arising from freedom from the cycle of birth and death. The word 'Paramananda' is composed of two words – 'Param' meaning ultimate and 'Ananda' which means happiness or bliss. So this is the ultimate state of happiness which arises from a deep seated permanent connection with the inner self. According to the Vedanta school of Hindu philosophy, Paramananda is that state of sublime delight when the 'Jiva', the individual empirical self, becomes free from all sins, all doubts, all desires, all actions, all pains, all sufferings and also all physical and mental ordinary pleasures, having become established in Brahman, the eternal Universal Self and the subtle essence underlying all existence, it becomes Jivanmukta, it becomes liberated.

To secure happiness, Hinduism prescribes a holistic method, which takes into consideration both the material and spiritual needs of human beings. It recognizes four chief aims of human life, called purusharthas, by pursuing which human beings can experience physical, mental, and spiritual happiness. They are also called the four chief purposes (purusharthas) of existence, because they are also chosen by God (Purusha) himself for his own enjoyment. They refer to religious and moral duty (dharma), wealth (artha), conjugal bliss (kama) and liberation (moksha). Let us examine how they contribute to our happiness. By pursuing dharma, you enjoy name and fame, social status, and respect in society. By pursuing wealth you enjoy the comforts of life, status in society, and the satisfaction of fulfilling your obligations to family and society. By pursuing kama (sex) you enjoy conjugal bliss, companionship with your spouse, family life, and the happiness of having children, relations, and continuation of family lineage. Finally, pursuing liberation, you can secure the ultimate happiness of being absolutely and eternally free from all obligations. For a human being, the four aims are the best means to secure happiness upon earth and lay a firm foundation for future happiness in the world of Brahman, the highest Self.

Human life has been further divided into four stages called 'Ashramas' which every human being should go through with specific goals and responsibilities for each stage:

- Brahmacharya – celibate student: This is the first stage of human life starting from the time a baby is born till the time the baby grows up and gets married. This stage emphasizes gaining knowledge by studying the ancient scriptures called Vedas and understanding ones duties and responsibilities (Dharma). In modern day life this corresponds to formal education and understanding and preparing for an adult life in a specific field of occupation which requires studying the relevant courses. Ancient scriptures emphasize the importance of sexual abstinence during this stage so that the student can fully focus on acquiring knowledge without any distractions.

- Grihasta - homemaker: After Brahmacharya comes the stage of Grihasta which literally means married life with the responsibilities of raising and nurturing a family while performing the professional duties for which one has studied during the Brahmacharya stage. At this stage Hinduism supports the pursuit of wealth as a means of rearing and nurturing the family and indulgence in sexual pleasure (called Kama in Sanskrit) under defined societal norms. Duties of a human being at this stage range from protecting the family, having children so that the family lineage (called Vansh) continues, ensuring children get educated with the right set of moral values, performing one's professional duties, ensuring the societal connections of the family are managed and the family contributes to society in a positive manner.

- Vanaprastha – hermit: The Girhastha stage ends when the person's children enter the Grihasta stage and start to lead an independent life with their respective nuclear family. In this stage the person has to retire into seclusion and contemplate upon his experiential wisdom (dharma) and the ultimate purpose of human life (liberation). At this age, he should renounce all physical, material and sexual pleasures, retire from his social and professional life, leave his home for a forest hut, where he can spend his time in prayers. He is allowed to take his spouse along but maintains little contact with the rest of the family.

- Sanyasa – Recluse: This is the last stage of human life where the person should be totally devoted to God. He has no home, no other attachments; he has renounced all desires, fears, hopes, duties, and responsibilities. He is virtually merged with God, all his worldly ties are broken, and his sole concern becomes attaining moksha or release from the circle of birth and death.

Christianity

Christianity also provides guidance on how people can be happier. There are multiple verses where happiness is mentioned and a path to happiness preached. I quote some verses here

"Happy are the people whose God is the Lord" Psalm 144:15

"Take delight in the Lord, and he will give you the desires of your heart" Psalm 37:4

"With joy you will draw water from the wells of salvation" Isaiah 12:3

"Blessed are the pure in heart, for they will see God" Matthew 5:8

"But rejoice inasmuch as you participate in the sufferings of Christ, so that you may be overjoyed when his glory is revealed" Peter 4:13

"How happy your people must be! How happy your officials, who continually stand before you and hear your wisdom" Chronicles 9:7

On World Youths' Day in 2015 Pope Francis said to youths - Christianity is not a set of prohibitions, but a "project for life" that can lead to true happiness in building better relationships and a better world. The Pope asked "Do you realise how much you are worth in the eyes of God? Do you know that you are loved and welcomed by him unconditionally?" The "beatitude" or blessedness for which God created human beings and which was disrupted by the sin of Adam and Eve "consists in perfect communion with God, with others, with nature and with ourselves," the pope wrote. God's "divine light was meant to illuminate every human relationship with truth and transparency."

But with sin, he said, Adam and Eve's relationship with each other, with God and with creation changed. "The inner compass which had guided them in their quest for happiness lost its point of reference and the attractions of power, wealth, possessions and a desire for pleasure at all costs led them to the abyss of sorrow and anguish."

God still loved the human creatures he created and still wanted them to find happiness, the pope said, so he send his son to become one of them and to redeem them.

Jesus taught that impurity or defilement was not something that happened because of what someone ate or who they touched, but was something that came from inside the person. Jesus listed "evil thoughts, fornication, theft, murder, adultery, coveting, wickedness, deceit, licentiousness, envy, slander, pride, foolishness," the pope said, pointing out that most of the things on the list have to do with a person's relationship with others.

"We need to show a healthy concern for creation, for the purity of our air, water and food," the pope told young people, "but how much more do we need to protect the purity of what is most precious of all: our heart and our relationships. This 'human ecology' will help us to breathe the pure air that comes from beauty, from true love, and from holiness."

Pope Francis said he knows "your desire for a love which is genuine, beautiful and expansive" is beginning to blossom. It is such a powerful gift of God that it must be protected and nurtured with care.

The ability to love and be loved is beautiful and is a key to happiness, but sin means it also can be "debased, destroyed or spoiled" by selfishness or the desire for pleasure or power, he said in the message, published by the Vatican.

d.   Culture and happiness

It is not surprising that like many religions, many cultures also profess happiness and provide guidance on how to lead more happy and fulfilling lives. Let us spend some time learning about how various cultures profess the practice of happiness

- Lagom (Sweden): Lagom pronounced 'Laaw-gum' literally means not too much, not too little – just enough. It encourages people to live life optimally avoiding extremes. In Sweden, citizens have a life expectancy two years longer than the OECD average. That could have something to do with the 37.5-hour work week, an average of 33 days of vacation per year and generous social safety net. Other contributors include it's clean air, good fishing, the mandatory breaks for coffee and cake and ofcourse the Lagom approach to life. The word Lagom is used as an adjective or adverb across all aspects of life describing the optimal or 'just right' approach to everything. In communication it means speaking just enough – sharing only as much information as needed, refraining from speaking ill and rarely giving gratuitous compliments. An associated concept of 'Jante' promotes collective success rather than individual brilliance. Compare this to American culture where individual bravado and achievements top everything else and everybody idolizes 'heroes' in all fields of life (media, sports, business, academic and others) for their superlative achievements. Extending this concept to dining and food habits means that Swedes eat just right – optimal portion sizes that carry adequate nutrition for the body promoting sustainable sources of food and avoid excesses. Swedish food habits promote purity, freshness, simplicity and balance. Like in many cultures food becomes a platform facilitating social interactions and the Swedes have given a specific name to 'taking a break with friends' and call it 'Fika' pronounced 'fee-car' which is the ritual of meeting friends over coffee and cinnamon buns often multiple times a day. This benefits people in multiple ways – not only do people step out from the stress of work, they meet friends and share their feelings over a comforting sip of comfort food - coffee and buns. This lowers stress levels, enhances self-image, reassures people that they have a safety net or support system of friends and prepares them for the upcoming part of the work day. Lagom extends to wellness and self care as well – Swedes like to live their lives outdoors in beautiful, clean, healthy natural surroundings, exercise well to keep a healthy body, rest and slow down from the daily hustle bustle of life adequately and indulge moderately in massages and sauna. In the business world the concept of lagom emphasizes shared success, enhanced teamwork and focus on consensus based decision making. In negotiation scenarios win-win situations are preferred to create sustainable and trust based relationships amongst business partners rather than one party taking all the gains at the expense of the other. For a country with a population less than 10 million people, Sweden has done exceedingly well in the business field with many successful global enterprises across different industry segments like the home and living powerhouse Ikea, the automotive wonder Volvo (now owned by Geely Motors), clothing and lifestyle brand H&M, tech startup Spotify and telecom major Ericsson to name a few.

- Hygge (Denmark)

Hygge pronounced 'hue-guh' means having a conscious appreciation for the present. In a country with less than 1700 hours of sunshine annually (compared with 2700 in Greece) life can get dreary, boring and depressing. The concept of Hygge was developed by Danes to create appreciation for the small things in life and creating simple acts in your daily routine which become rituals to drive happiness regularly. Hygge also encourages the creation of a cozy environment around us to make daily life enjoyable, comfortable and pleasurable. The obvious space which is most in our control is our home. Hygge emphasizes creation of very 'homely' living spaces a cocoon where we feel truly relaxed, which helps us rejuvenate, helps us introspect and think about life and creates an environment of overall well being. There are multiple ways of doing this – sufficiently lit rooms, use of candles, beautiful sleek lamps, wide and open rooms, a fireplace to create warmth, and making a special corner called hyggekrog a special personal space where you can cosy up, relax, read a book or just enjoy a warm drink. While the creation of a cozy comfortable home is something that can be accomplished over a weekend, the day to day practice of hygge and the appreciation of the small things in life is something that takes practice and constant attention. In the end, Hygge is about being content with what you have, reminding yourself constantly about the small treasures you have, creating a comfortable cocoon where you feel safe and rejuvenate and creating and creating and relishing small positive happiness impulses like lighting a candle, buying a flower, stopping by at the local café for a short chat.

- Ikigai (Japan)

Ikigai literally translates into 'reason for existence'. It questions our motivation, our talents, the demand for those talents in the world we live in and how much are these talents valued monetarily by the world. It reminds me about the concept of supply and demand in economics and meshes it beautifully with our natural ability for some tasks and what we are passionate about in life.

It also prescribes a way of life that enhances health, happiness and longevity. It is not surprising that this comes from Okinawa, Japan an area with the highest life expectancy in the world. Dan Buettner identified 5 areas where people live the longest and called these areas Blue Zones – the term first used in 2005 in a National Geographic magazine cover story. The other 4 areas are: Sardinia (Italy); Nicoya (Costa Rica); Icaria (Greece) and Loma Linda, California. Lets go a little deeper into Ikigai and the advice that the oldest residents of Okinawa give for a long healthy life – 1. Optimism: Okinawa was bombed during the world war and more than two hundred thousand lives were lost. The community bounced back from this massive setback and remains highly optimistic about life in general. Inspirational positive quotes from residents of this region help them and the people around them remain youthful in old age. 2. Physical activity: residents of Okinawa are physically active throughout the day. They don't go to the gym and do rigorous physical exercise but they have integrated physical activity in their daily routines – working in the garden, nature walks, daily gentle body mind soul exercises like Tai Chi, Yoga and Shiatsu in the morning. 3. Healthy eating: Okinawans, research has shown, eat a diet rich in vegetables and herbs, and low in animal products. Daily staples, like seaweed, sweet potatoes, green tea and miso, are high in antioxidants. Okinawans consume one-third as much sugar and nearly half as much salt as the rest of Japan. Locals, the authors note, eat a wide variety of foods, especially vegetables and spices—an average of 18 different foods a day. They also consume fewer calories—1,758 per day compared to 2,068 in the rest of Japan and an estimated 2,200 to 3,300 calories in the U.S. The Okinawan diet is built around nutrient-dense, low-calorie vegetables and fruits. They also subscribe to the Japanese concept of hara hachi bu, which means "fill your belly to 80 percent." In other words, stop eating before you feel completely full. 4. Community: Okinawans have strong social bonds within the local community. It is not uncommon for octogenarians to go for a walk to the seaside in the morning and stop for morning tea at a neighbour's place on the way back. They also regularly organize social events like karaoke, gateball competitions, birthday parties all organized by local residents for local residents. They have few restaurants and no bars – residents usually go to each other's homes to spend time together.

- Ubuntu (Africa)

Ubuntu in South African literally means human kindness. It professes a strong bond among humans and the existence of humans because of this strong bond with each other. Simply inferred – it means a human is a human through other humans. Unity amongst humans and caring for each other through good times and bad is the core essence of Ubuntu. Positive social impact is what humans should strive for in their lives and by doing this they become happy themselves and create happiness in the society that they are a part of. "If you want to go fast, go alone. If you want to go far, go together as a group". That ancient African proverb is expressed in the Ubuntu ethics or philosophy when it speaks about living in community. Ubuntu became known in the West largely through the writings of Desmond Tutu, the archbishop of Cape Town who was a leader of the anti-apartheid movement and who won the Nobel Peace Prize for his work. In this day and age of 'I, me, myself' catalyzed by technology driven social alienation Ubuntu is a reminder that we all belong to a larger group of people like us and being part of this social fabric is what makes us us. Although South Africa as a country is ranked #116 in the United Nations' Global Happiness Index this concept I feel is something that we can all learn from and imbibe in our daily lives.

- Keyif (Turkey)

Keyif is roughly translatable as 'a pleasurable state of idle relaxation'. The pursuit of idle pleasure is a national pastime in Turkey. Originally an Arabic term signifying 'mood, contentment, intoxication', the word has become truly international, with variations of it found in Russian, Persian, Turkish, Hebrew, Kurdish, Urdu, Hindi, and various Central Asian languages. This is an individual affair where each one of us has to find our 'keyif' moment – a time when we disconnect with everything around us, look inside, relax and take refuge from the stress of life and just rejuvenate. It can simply be having a tea in a quiet café, or listening to our favourite song on a beautiful lakeside or reading a book. The closest corresponding English term would be 'taking a break' but it doesn't capture the rejuvenation aspect of this ritual. I would call it lazy bohemianism – carefree, uninterrupted, rejuvenating power breaks.

- Brazil

Brazil was ranked 28th in the World Happiness Report 2018 – much higher than other BRICS (Brazil, Russia, India, China and South Africa) countries who are considered to be economically similar. The next ranked was Russia at 59 – worse by a factor higher than 2. In Brazil living well and being happy is so well engrained in day to day life they didn't need to coin a term for it. Lets call it 'Brazilianism' – what is it exactly and what can we learn about happiness from this young nation centered in the heart of the Amazonian rainforests. Social inclusion of diverse ethnicities and races, healthy lifestyle and celebration at a larger than life scale are key to happiness in this country. Social diversity and inclusion of people from indigenous, Nigerian, Portuguese, Italian, German, Japanese and Korean ancestry are all common making Brazilians a truly unique mix. It is noteworthy that Brazil has the second highest population of people of African descent. Brazil is truly a melting pot of diverse cultures, races, ethnicities each being an integrated part of the social fabric living peacefully with each other. Brazilians are also very physically active – more than 70% of the population exercises for more than 1 hour per week. Their prowess globally in sports like Football (or Soccer for my American friends) and volleyball is well known. Other sports popularly played in Brazil are futevolei, Capoeira, jiu-jitsu and polo – not to mention exercising in a gym. Brazil has the world's second largest fitness industry. All this results in dramatically lower average weight and BMI than in the U.S. According to government data, the average height and weight of a 30-something Brazilian man is 5'6" and 163.5 pounds (a BMI of 26.3) and a woman, 5'2" and 137 pounds (25.1 BMI), compared to the U.S., where a comparable man is 5'9" and 199.5 pounds (29.5 BMI) and woman is 5'4" and 169 pounds

(29 BMI). This leads to much lower obesity levels, less visits to the doctor, lowered stress levels and ultimately a happier life. Brazilians could also easily be declared world champions in celebrating – the Carnival is unlike any other celebration in the world dwarfing everything else with its size, scope and duration. The wonderful processions with colorful dancers dancing to the beats of samba is a feat that has to be seen to be believed. But it is not only the Carnival that Brazilians celebrate – they turn all occasions ranging from São Joao to réveillon into spectacles of communal togetherness and joy.

- India

Arguably the oldest civilization in the world and home to one sixth of the world's population Indian culture deeply embeds the pursuit of happiness as a daily activity that goes unnoticed by millions. Yoga was developed in India and is now one of the most widely adopted wellness practices around the world. It incorporates breathing exercises, meditation and physical poses which brings many benefits like – lower stress levels, increased flexibility, weight control and a better sex life. Eating habits in India revolve around a largely vegetarian diet (80% of the population is Hindu) which is linked with increased longevity, lower risk of diabetes, heart disease and high blood pressure. Indian cooking is also rich in spices like turmeric which are known to have anti-inflammatory, anti-carcinogenic, anti-fungal and anti-bacterial qualities. They ward off diseases and strengthen the immune system. Indians also have very strong family ties and consider it to be the primary social unit. Till today many people live together in so called joint families which are multiple nuclear families living under one roof sharing the burdens of life and enjoying the pleasures of life together. They eat meals cooked in a common kitchen and often contribute to a central fund to run the household managed by one person in the family. This becomes a self-fulfilled integrated social unit where each person contributes to society with his or her special skills. The elderly get the care they need from family members, children benefit from the knowledge and love from the elderly and working adults don't need to hire childcare or elderly care services to take care of children alone at home. Life's expenses get split up between various contributing members and this reduces financial burden. The big compromise though is loss of individuality and privacy and the pursuit of individual goals and activities. This has led to the proliferation in nuclear families and the adoption of a western lifestyle. Indians also celebrate various festivals and have the highest number of public holidays in the world at 21 since it is home to various religions and cultures as people from all over the world migrated to India over the last centuries and settled down permanently calling it home. From the Hindu festivals of Holi and Diwali to the Christian festivities of Christmas – all festivals are celebrated with equal fervor and joyousness.

HappSys

We have by now read about what drives happiness, how different religions and cultures view happiness and profess its practice. You may, by now, say some of these ideas or concepts work for you – some don't, some you would naturally do, some you would have to be pushed to do and some you wouldn't do at all.

We are all unique – each one of us has a different biological, psychological, cultural, socio-political, economic and physical composition. I would like to explore the concept of 'individual identity' here before I introduce my HappSys system of living a happy life to you.

Before we attempt to develop a system for you it is important for you to understand who you are. What is your 'identity'? What is it that makes you 'you'? Psychologists have studied the concept of identity since the early 1900s and there is a ton of scientific research on this topic. I will not go too much in academic details and will try and simplify it for you. In psychology identity relates to self-image, self-esteem and individuality.

Self-image:

Self-image in its most basic form is a mental picture you have of yourself. Its how you think and feel about yourself. This picture is formed over time and changes as you gain life experiences. There are multiple contributing factors to this picture – how you see yourself, how do other people see yourself, and how do you think other people see yourself. This is a complex assimilation based partially on what you think others think you are and is therefore subject to a fair amount of bias (both positive and negative), self-criticism, prejudice and the kind of life experiences you have had growing up. Social influence plays a key role in contributing to your self-image – think about all the people you interact with, all the magazines and reading material you are exposed to, all the shows you watch on TV or streaming services, all the chatter on social media – all of this influences your self-image. *Collective paradigms* are shared rules, assumptions, boundaries, standards, evaluations, beliefs and limitations that we have come to accept and adopt over time. They shape how we think, what we say, how we do things, and the perspectives we hold about relationships, friendships, people, career, health, business, religion, etc Think of this as the framework that has evolved over time and exists within which your belief system operates. Collective paradigm is not necessarily the truth or scientific fact but is the most widely accepted consensus view of things. Before it was discovered that earth was round everybody believed they were living on a flat plate. There are some things that we accept as normal – like getting an education or skills to be able to find employment, having to work to earn a living, working during the day and sleeping at night, following rules and norms set by society.

Social influence has a big role in creating self-image. We do a lot of things solely because we see people around us do that or because people around us ask us to do that. Think of buying the same kind of clothes the 'cool' kids in school wore to be accepted by that group. It's important to also take into consideration cultural indoctrination. Your cultural and religious backgrounds are built upon certain beliefs, perspectives, and traditions. All of these things influence how you think, what you say, and the decisions you make, or the decisions you choose not to make on a daily basis.

Personal influence comes from every experience you have made in life - positive or negative – over the years, all the successes and failures, all the knowledge you have gained over time. The interesting thing is that self-image is not based on actual facts but the way you interpret and have stored these experiences. False memories are just as powerful as real memories. Both types will significantly influence your choices, thoughts, and perspectives in the present moment — for better or worse.

"It's not what you say out of your mouth that determines your life, it's what you whisper to yourself that has the most power" – Robert Kiyosaki

Self esteem:

In psychology, the term self-esteem is used to describe a person's overall sense of self-worth or personal value. In other words, how much you appreciate and like yourself. Self-esteem is often seen as a personality trait, which means that it tends to be stable and enduring. Self-esteem can involve a variety of beliefs about yourself, such as the appraisal of your own appearance, beliefs, emotions, and behaviors. Self-esteem can play a significant role in your motivation and success throughout your life. Low self-esteem may hold you back from succeeding at school or work because you don't believe yourself to be capable of success. By contrast, having a healthy self-esteem can help you achieve because you navigate life with a positive, assertive attitude and believe you can accomplish your goals.

Individuality:

An individual is an indivisible person who exists as a unique entity. Despite being part of a social group, a family, an individual possesses his or her own desires and aspirations, needs and wants, psychological and physical characteristics, own thoughts and views and this is what makes each of you different and special. John Locke in 17th century Britian introduced the idea of the individual as a blank slate (tabula rasa) shaped from birth by life's experiences including education, family ties, social environment, political beliefs, economic environment etc.

It is for this reason that each one of us is unique. In a study of genetically identical mice in Germany in 2013, it was concluded that they could develop very different personalities. The researchers identified a link between exploratory behavior in the young mice and the birth of new neurons in their brains during adulthood. The mice were both genetically identical and living in the same maze-like environment with twists, turns, and toys. Researchers equipped the mice with a special microchip emitting electromagnetic signals, which allowed the scientists to track the mice's movements and to rate their exploratory behavior. Despite a common environment and identical genes, the mice showed highly individual patterns of behavior. They reacted to their environment differently, and throughout the three-month experiment those differences increased. Most importantly, some mice traveled and explored a wider area than others did. The difference in personality was attributed to the generation of neurons due to exploration of larger areas by some mice. This study was instrumental in exhibiting that personal experiences help shape how the brain reacts to new information and leads to the development of new behaviors going forward.

In conclusion it is safe to say that each one of us is different despite all the commonalities we may have. Therefore, to assume that one approach will fit the needs of all is not only naïve it is oversimplifying the concept of individuality.

Know yourself – Life Journey

Planet Earth has 6 billion people – despite that, no two are the same. This difference comes from our unique journeys in life. Where we were born, what kind of a family we were raised in, what kind of people have been around us and what kind of people we choose to be with now, what kind of education we have acquired, what were our areas of interest and hobbies, what are our professional fields, what are our political interests, what our personal lives are like, what external events have had an impact on us, our physical health and mental well being, our conscious and unconsciously done mistakes, our values and beliefs, our hopes and fears, our trials and tribulations, financial and socio-economic condition and outlook and a multitude of these experiences and events make us all unique. One in six billion unique! No manufactured product on Earth has been produced six billion times and the principle of economies of scale means that all products produced in large quantities have to be identical – however in God's factory (if we can call it that) each human produced is unique. This is exactly why no single approach to happiness can be applicable to such a diverse and large group of people. Each one of us has to have an approach that is customized to our unique personality, our unique LifeJourney and our unique set of needs and desires.

The millions of day to day interactions we have with our surroundings – people, places, objects and the impact it has on our minds and bodies makes us who we are today. All these experiences have an impact on us and condition us towards the way we deal with situations now. Some events have a bigger impact than others. For example if you were bullied in school for an elongated period of time it is probably going to have a bigger impact than an accidental fall from your bicycle resulting in minor scratches. Growing up seeing your parents fighting with each other all the time may reduce your belief in the institution of family and marriage; conversely, growing up in a family with healthy relations between your parents will reinforce your belief in these institutions. There are thousands of pages of scientific research on which events cause the maximum stress and which events are the happiest events for most people and I will synthesize this tone of research into a couple of pages and make it easy for you.

Stressful events - The Holmes And Rahe Stress Scale

Thomas Holmes and Richard Rahe studied medical records of 5000 patients in 1967 and found that a strong correlation did exist between stressful events in life and the possibility of getting ill. This correlation was so strong that they ranked stressful situations on a scale from most stressful to least stressful.

1. Death of a spouse (or child): 100
2. Divorce: 73
3. Marital separation: 65
4. Imprisonment: 63
5. Death of a close family member: 63
6. Personal injury or illness: 53
7. Marriage: 50
8. Dismissal from work: 47
9. Marital reconciliation: 45
10. Retirement: 45

Happy events

A study was conducted among people above the age of 70 about the moments in life where they experienced pure happiness. The top 10 list is as follows:

1. Birth of a first child
2. Wedding day
3. Birth of grandchildren
4. Birth of another child
5. Day of retirement
6. Moving into a new home
7. Seeing your child's first steps
8. Hearing your child's first words
9. Meeting the person of your dreams
10. First kiss with the person you love

I would like to reiterate that all academic/scientific research has a specific scope and its limitations – for example the study is conducted upon people from a certain country which the researchers belong to or certain age group, or certain commonality like profession or medical condition or life experience, restricted by sample size etc. Therefore, what makes you super happy or super sad may not be on the above lists. It does not need to be -

because you are unique. Hence, it is imperative that we draft out YOUR LifeJourney and identify your individual triggers of happiness and sadness – just a few minutes and we are there (I know you have been waiting for long).

What is also important is seeing how the people closest to us – grandparents, parents, family, friends, teachers, coaches, coworkers, neighbours respond to events in their life. The people around us shape us as individuals. Let us look at how the people around us influence us in a bit more detail – I will choose five specific sets of people impacting us in different stages of life:

- Influence of grandparents on children

The relationship between grandparents and grandchildren is a special one – I can probably write a book on this topic as I have personally gained so much from my grandparents – for now let us focus on the key aspects. Grandparents can act as an authority figure who provide unconditional love. This gives the child the first positive feedback from authority figures in general which goes a long way in the developmental process. When extended to other authority figures that the child will face in life like teachers, coaches, peers in authority positions this can reduce the anxiety of a child when preparing to have their first interaction with the authority figure hoping that just like their grandparents accepted them so will the new authority figure. Provision of unconditional love also makes grandparents the least risky and most reliable and trustworthy figure to go to for emotional support. Children realize that grandparents will accept their flaws as much as they appreciate the positives in children. Grandparents also usually have more time and patience than working biological parents. When this time and patience is invested into teaching grandchildren skills like reading, writing, gardening, sports or other activities this can be a very fulfilling learning experience for children. Grandparents with their storytelling also help children understand their family background and history which creates a sense of pride, belongingness and a solid foundation and further inspires children to develop into successful people with good moral values achieving results which are better (or at least at par) with previous generations. Grandparents share their wisdom acquired in their own lives over decades of positive and negative experiences – providing children with their first acquired instinctive responses to certain situations they may face in their lives. Grandparents also put the small issues in perspective like having forgotten to do homework on a day and calm down hyper-nerves of children. They encourage children to look at the big picture with their broader world view. In today's world where grandparents and grandchildren are usually living in different cities or even countries technology is providing ways of keeping this bond alive and strong. With FaceTime, Skype, Watsapp or other videoconferencing applications grandparents can find ways of spending more time with their grandkids.

- Influence of parents on children

This is quite an obvious one. Parents (biological or foster) are the first reference point of the world for children. Children absorb everything they see in their parents – choice of words, choice of clothes, tone of talking, eating habits, social skills, goal setting in professional lives, the list is endless. Children incorporate all of these things in their own lives. The World Health Organization (WHO) defines child health as follows: "Child health is a state of physical, mental, intellectual, social and emotional well-being and not merely the absence of disease or infirmity. Healthy children live in families, environments and communities that provide them with the opportunity to reach their fullest developmental potential."

Clearly, parents have a primary role to play in all aspects of the above definition. There is also strong evidence of negative influences on children - in 2011, the UK's Department for Education found that children who are exposed to bad parenting are two times more likely to misbehave. Inconsistent and harsh parenting styles can lead to children developing anti-social tendencies, poor resilience to changes in life (changing schools, finding new friends, relocating to a new city, new teacher in class), depression and/or higher levels of anger leading to increased display of aggression. Since many of us are parents, I will elaborate on what we can do in our parenting roles to provide our children the right conditions to thrive and succeed in. Parents of successful children have the following things in common:

1. They make their kids do chores: By making kids do chores – like cleaning up after playing, taking out the garbage, cleaning their shoes, doing laundry, doing the dishes, gardening children realize they have to do the work in life to be able to create a better life for themselves and everybody around them. This gives them a sense of responsibility and that they have to contribute to the larger ecosystem around them

2. Teaching social skills: Researchers from Pennsylvania State University and Duke University tracked more than 700 children from across the US between kindergarten and age 25 and found a significant correlation between their social skills as kindergartners and their success as adults two decades later. Children with better social skills were more likely to get a college degree and have a full time job by the age of 25

3. High expectations: Parents who have high expectations from their children have a huge impact on the attainment of these goals. The Pygmalion effect states "that what one person expects of another can come to serve as a self-fulfilling prophecy" – for kids they try their best to live up to the expectations of their parents

4. Have healthy relations with each other: Children in high conflict families fare worse than children of parents who get along well

5. Parents are well educated themselves: A 2014 study lead by University of Michigan psychologist Sandra Tang found that mothers who finished high school or college were more likely to raise kids that did the same

6. Teach kids math: According to Northwestern University researcher Greg Duncan mastery of early math skills predicts not only future match achievement it also predicts future reading achievement

7. Strong relationship with kids: Parents developing a strong relationship with kids till the age of three provide a secure base for kids to explore the world thereby increasing chances of their success

8. Get less stressed: Parents, especially mothers, who manage stress better or get less stressed avoid unknowingly transferring this feeling of stress to their children. Emotional contagion means if parents get less stressed in front of kids, kids will be exposed to this negativity less and will have a higher feeling of security

9. They value effort over innate ability: Parents of successful children focus on developing and improving skill sets of their children and prepare them for specific challenges. They do not reward kids' success by saying "you are born intelligent hence you succeeded." They make sure children realize that skills can be improved when practiced and no one is born

with a specific set of qualities that sets them
up for success in the future

10. Mothers work: According to research out of
Harvard Business School, there are significant
benefits for children growing up with mothers
who work outside the home. The study found
daughters of working mothers went to school
longer, were more likely to have a job in a
supervisory role, and earned more money —
23% more compared to their peers who were
raised by stay-at-home mothers. The sons of
working mothers also tended to pitch in more
on household chores and childcare, the study
found — they spent seven-and-a-half more
hours a week on childcare and 25 more
minutes on housework.

11. Higher socioeconomic status: "Drive" author
Dan Pink has noted, the higher the income for
the parents, the higher the SAT scores for the
kids. "Absent comprehensive and expensive
interventions, socioeconomic status is what
drives much of educational attainment and
performance," he wrote.

12. They teach 'grit': Grit is defined as a
"tendency to sustain interest in and effort
toward very long-term goals" – its about
teaching kids to imagining and committing to
work towards a future that they want to create
for themselves (inspired by the high goals set
by parents)

- Influence of spouses on each other

Spousal relationship is a unique relationship. It combines elements from various other relationships – nurturing and protecting aspect of parenting, helping and supporting aspects from siblings, open communication and exploration of new experiences from friendship, trust and caring aspect from grandparents, building together (e.g. having babies together, building a house together) and joint risk taking aspects from business partners, sexual and physical intimacy – this makes this relationship special and unique. When all these elements are combined over a prolonged duration in your lives – this becomes one of the most important if not the most important relationship of your life. So what impact does this relationship have on our lives. I will skip the steps of falling in love and the part of establishment of this relationship and focus more on what happens after this is established.

A study conducted by Michigan State university looked at about 2,000 older married heterosexual couples from 2006 to 2012 and found that those who reported a happier spouse also reported feeling better overall – people with a happy partner are 34% more likely to be healthier. Happy spouses exude higher levels of energy and affection, and coax and cajole their partners into adopting healthier lifestyle habits like exercising, eating healthy and taking better care of themselves. Happy partners make life easy or atleast make it seem easy which leads to greater satisfaction and well being in the other partner so they are more likely to avoid self-destructive behavior like substance abuse or alcoholism. Behavioral contagion is a well known fact that we have discussed earlier in the book and it is most applicable with life partners.

Psychiatrists at the University of Toronto studied the relationship between medical health and a happy marriage – couples in happy marriages report lower blood pressure and thinner heart walls. Effects are not limited to cardiovascular systems alone – it impacts the immune system, gastrointestinal problems and emotional disorders – basically every system that can be impacted with the way a person handles stress. Quoting studies in various countries like Sweden and the U.S. – people in a satisfying spousal relationship live longer, have less depression, less anxiety disorders, fewer phobias, fewer accidents and a reduced likelihood of dying from cancer, heart disease and most killer diseases. Another study completed in 2015 by the "National Bureau of Economic Research" reports, "Those whose spouse or partner is also considered their best friend get almost twice as much additional life satisfaction from marriage or cohabitation as do others."

When relationships dissolve the process gets reversed completely – in the bereavement process people secrete huge amounts of the stress chemical cortisol and the body becomes susceptible to different kinds of diseases and infections. Combining this with a lowered will to live increases the chances of death significantly.

We discussed good spousal relationships – but what about bad ones. Penn state researchers studied 1150 participants over a 12 year duration and found that people who remain unhappily married suffer from lower levels of self-esteem, overall health, overall happiness, and life satisfaction along with elevated levels of psychological distress, in contrast to those in long-term happy marriages. Individuals in unhappy marriages do not reap benefits related to overall happiness, life satisfaction, self-esteem, and health, typically associated with marriage. Those who are unhappily married are not obtaining the social and emotional support available to individuals from marriage. We know that divorce is the second most stressful event of life but for people in bad marriages research suggests that it is better to dissolve the marriage and start afresh. Despite the negative consequences of divorce that lower people's psychological well-being, there is some evidence that remaining unhappily married is more detrimental than divorcing. Individuals who divorce and remain unmarried have greater life satisfaction and higher levels of self-esteem and overall health than unhappily married individuals.

- Influence of friends on teenagers

Teen years are a very important stage of development for human beings. This is the transitionary stage between childhood and adulthood and a lot of important aspects of life get established in these years. Self-image, self-esteem, social relations, romantic and sexual relations and a platform for professional future are all established during these years.

Teenagers spend more time with friends than any other social contacts including parents and siblings. Teenagers want to bond with their friends and impress them and therefore friends influence many aspects of a teenager's life. If friends are impressed by getting good grades then the person will try and excel academically. On the contrary, if friends are impressed by drinking or substance abuse it will provide the teenager with motivation to be attracted towards and attempt such activities. Teenagers develop their own identity by being part of this peer group. The peer group influences many choices the person makes ranging from the type of clothes, to the choice of activities outside and in school, communication style and content etc. According to Statista, Friends are the second most influential social group when it comes to decisions about sex after parents.

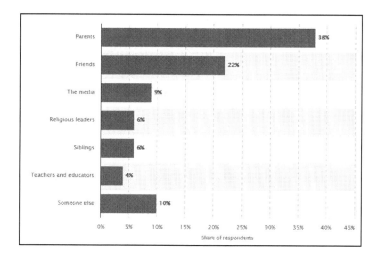

Peer pressure is a buzzword when it comes to teenagers or adolescents. Peer influence is when you choose to do something you wouldn't otherwise do, because you want to feel accepted and valued by your friends. It isn't just or always about doing something against your will. You might hear the term 'peer pressure' used a lot. But peer influence is a better way to describe how teenagers' behaviour is shaped by wanting to feel they belong to a group of friends or peers. Coping well with peer influence is about finding the right balance between being yourself and fitting in with your group.

- Influence of bosses/managers in the workplace on adults

Working adults spend more active time in the office than they do at home. On average full time employed people spend 8-10 hours per day in the office, 1-3hours travelling to and fro, an hour to get ready, 3-4 hours for food and leisure, 6-10 hours of sleep and the remaining time for miscellaneous activities. The time spent in office constitutes 50% of our active daily life – half of our life (where we do something apart from sleeping) is spent in the office! It is spent in the company of our co-workers and the one person who has direct influence on this time is the manager or boss. This person directly controls or at the least strongly influences how much you earn, what are your chances of progressing further in the company/career and how this person treats you directly has an impact on your day to day happiness. I cannot recollect anybody telling me they were super happy after getting into an altercation with their manager. The reason for this is clear - most people rely on their primary occupation for earning their livelihood and the 8-10 hours spent in office are important to the financial well-being, career advancement and self-image of themselves and to an extent also their families. With so much depending upon this one relationship - it influences our day to day happiness levels. Appreciation from the boss makes you happy and criticism makes you sad.

Another aspect of this relationship is a bridge between the conflicting trends of employees staying in their jobs longer (Yes – as opposed to the myth of younger people being job hoppers) and the lifespan of companies getting shorter. Lets clarify these points with some eye opening data. First, are modern day employees less loyal and changing jobs more often? According to research from the U.S. Bureau of Labor Statistics, employees today stay longer with a company than they did 25 years ago. In 1983, the average employee tenure was around 3.5 years. Fifteen years later, in 1998, people stayed on the job an average of 3.6 years before leaving. In 2014, the average employee stayed 4.6 years

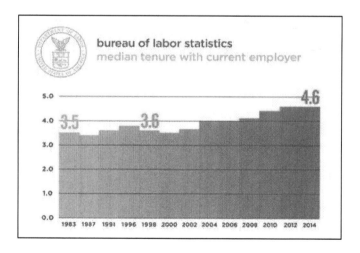

The U.K. shows a similar trend – although self-employment has increased, job separation has decreased.

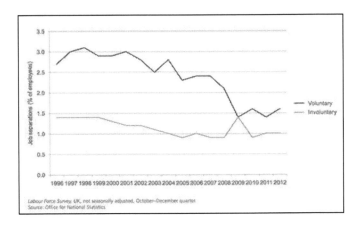

The above data points shatter the myth that employees change jobs more frequently and are less 'loyal' than employees earlier. This clearly shows that employees still want to build lasting relationships with their employers and would like to stay on and develop themselves within their existing companies. There is however another problem – companies themselves are dying quicker than ever! A study conducted by strategy consulting firm InnoSight shows the average tenure of companies in the S&P 500 has reduced from 33 years in 1965 to 20 years in 1990 and is forecasted to further shrink to 14 years by 2026. If we look at the largest companies in the world by market capitalization today and compare that to the beginning of this century – the results are astonishing

Global Rank (By market capitalization)	2018 (Market cap as of March 31st 2018)	2001
1	Apple	General Electric
2	Alphabet (Parent of Google)	Microsoft
3	Microsoft	Exxon
4	Amazon	Citi
5	Tencent	Walmart

Only 1 company (Microsoft) has managed to remain in the top 5. Alphabet (parent company of Google) and Tencent were both founded in the year 1998 – in just 20 years they have progressed from getting started to becoming the top 5 most valued companies in the world. While the lifespan of companies is reducing the working life of adults is increasing. According to Eurostat, the average working life in European countries increased from ~33 years in 2000 to ~36 years in 2016.

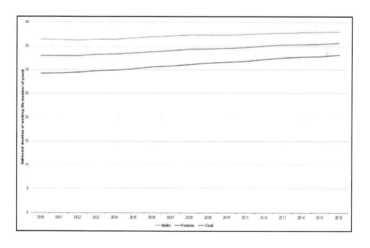

So people are working longer and lives of companies are getting shorter – despite wanting to stay in a company for longer people are switching jobs every 4.6 years. Why do people switch jobs? According to a LinkedIn survey in 2015, 46% people switched jobs when they did not have advancement opportunities and 41% switched jobs because they were dissatisfied with leadership (largely immediate boss).

Top reasons why people left their old job:

Reason	Percentage
I was concerned about the lack of opportunities for advancement	45%
I was unsatisfied with the leadership of senior management	41%
I was unsatisfied with the work environment / culture	36%
I wanted more challenging work	36%
I was unsatisfied with the compensation / benefits	34%
I was unsatisfied with the rewards/ recognition for my contributions	32%

Source: Linkedin survey. Why & How People Change Jobs. (Mar 2015). Showing global average.

Good bosses increase motivation levels of employees, lead to better performance and infuse their positive attitude in their teams – if you are managing people this advice should help you. If you have a boss, if you can have a harmonious relation with your boss and can find ways to develop your career further in the same company you will avoid a stressful event in life that significantly decreases happiness levels.

To be able to understand what will make us happier it is important to understand who we truly are. To be able to do that it is important we trace our individual life journeys – ive developed a patented system of doing this that allows you the flexibility to adapt this tool to your specific needs and at the same time create a visual map of how your life has been. Who are the key people who have influenced you? What are the key events that have shaped you as a person? What were some of your biggest victories? When did you feel the lowest? What is it that drives you as a person? What are behaviors that you don't like? What kind of people do you like – and which people do you don't like having around? What is it that you repent doing? What would you change in your past if you could get the chance to change it?

In short - What is it that makes you, YOU?

LifeJourney has two elements – form and content. Form is the format, layout and design of the tool and I will show you some options in a little while. Content is what goes into the format – these are your experiences and we will talk about that in detail as well. Let us now look at some forms of depicting your LifeJourney:

1. Phased approach

In this approach, you will divide your life into phases or eras. Each phase is a block of years or a stage of life that provides you with a clear delineation between them. It does not have to be a fixed number of years or scientifically defined development phases of human beings but your personal growth phases. For example, if you do not recollect much from the age of 5 to 15, then leave that out or just write a sentence about that phase. Focus on spans of time that were significant and shaped you as an individual. Let us look at the various formats you can use here

Figure x: LifeJourney – Phased Journey – Template 1

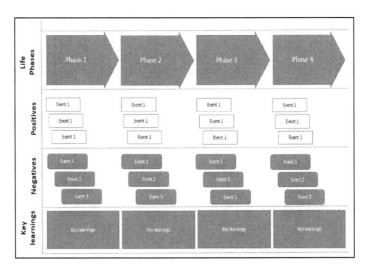

Figure x: LifeJourney – Phased Journey – Template 2

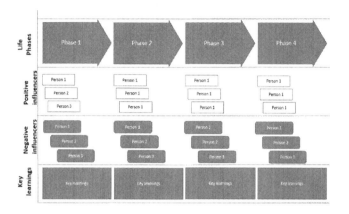

You can customize the template to add more phases in life. Ideally you should draw this on an A1 sized paper and use multiple sheets if needed. Don't restrict yourself by the size of the paper – this is your life – it may not fit into a single A1 sized sheet. Use the colors that you like – use red for negatives, green for positives, blue for key learnings. Make it visually appealing to you. Take time to work on it – make a first draft – then add to it, then revisit it after a week and add to it again if needed. First work on it alone – because you know best what affected you the most. Then, discuss it with a few people who know you well and who have shared your life with you – it could be siblings, parents, teachers, friends, pastors, preachers, coaches, spouses, coworkers, bosses, exes – be selective, choose carefully, you don't want anyone to trivialize this personal quest of yours. Ask them for their inputs – how did they see you evolve, what did they like about you in which phase, what did they did not like about you, try and correlate changes in your behavior and personality with key events or experiences.

Add more rows to make it more comprehensive – key behaviors exhibited, financial status, popularity, social status, professional status, geographical location, choice of music, choice of sports, hobbies, key habits – keep adding till it becomes a true snapshot of your life. It will be an emotional process, a process of deep introspection where you will be forced to confront your deepest sorrows and relive your biggest victories. If you in the habit of writing a daily diary – this LifeJourney will be a pictorial snapshot of your diary – something that you can read in a minute like the trailer of an interesting movie – just that this is the movie about your life where you are the protagonist.

2. Meandering river

Many people who I have worked with during the course of writing this book find the phased approach limiting or restricting the story telling process about their lives. A more continual approach is better suited for them – this led to the evolution of the meandering river template. A free flowing, continuous ongoing story about your life that flows like a river. When confronted with an obstacle the river finds its way around it and continues to flow – like life in general. Let us see how the template for the meandering river looks like

Figure x: LifeJourney – Meandering river – Template

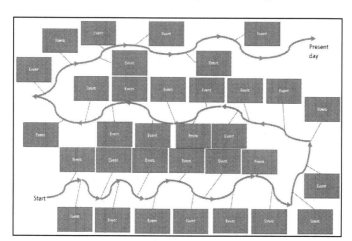

As you can see this is a freely flowing way of going through your life, highlighting what has been important to you and what incidents and experiences and which people have contributed to the creation of your present day personality. Just like in the Phased journey – feel free to spice this up with notable people, other observations, make it colorful, make it lively, add other notable aspects like location etc and customize it to truly reflect your LifeJourney and yourself as a person.

3. Highs and lows

In contrast to looking at the entire story it is also possible to look only at the defining moments – what were the times when you were riding high and what were the times when you felt that life handed you lemons. The Highs and Lows focusses on the extremities of your life on the positive and negative side and through these defining moments captures the core of your life. Each of us have some moments where we reveal aspects of our true character – either the positive or the negative side.

This does not mean that our response to a similar situation in the future will be the same – it can be entirely different and this is called character building. If you were unable to stand up for your family during a time of adversity and that is something which you truly repent it is not necessary that the next time you face a similar situation your response cannot change. You may be able to, by virtue of analyzing your LifeJourney and understanding your inner strengths and developed self be able to fight against your inner demons and give a totally contrarian response to the situation. This is the whole ethos of human life – learning from our limitations, building our strengths, channelizing our inner energy and transforming ourselves into better beings capable of managing bigger and more complex tasks and situations, capable of thwarting off bigger threats and living grander lives. Let us look at the template for Highs and Lows LifeJourney

Figure x: LifeJourney – Highs and lows – Template

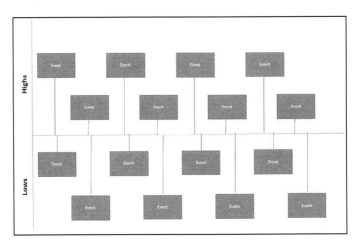

There are many ways of trying to extract the 'so-what' from the Highs and Lows template – you can identify a pattern and club together events of a similar nature or events where you have exhibited similar behaviors. You can map events to related people and look for patterns – which people always made you happy, who made you sad and caused grief. Try to go a level deeper – try to analyse in hindsight why they behaved that way – what could have been the circumstances that made them decide that way? What would have motivated them to do what they did? Was their behavior the expected behavior or a departure from their normal behavior? Did you do something which was unexpected that triggered this reaction from them? Were you behaving normally? This again will be an iterative process – make a first draft and then go back at it again multiple times to be able to make a holistic picture.

4. Quadrant of life

The quadrant of life approach allows us to very rapidly identify key events in our lives and the role that influencers have played in those events. Most events in our lives that have a profound impact on us involve interactions with other people – and often it is the role that others play that determines whether an incident becomes a positive or a negative memory. While we cannot control how others behave in specific situations, learning from past interactions can help us analyze what kind of people contributed positively to our development and what kind of people we should have avoided in our lives.

Figure x: LifeJourney – Quadrant of life – Template

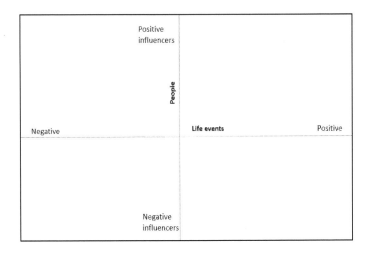

The quadrant of life is a synthesized version of first level of data – this requires you to pinpoint unique events and the role that various people played in those events. In many ways this allows us to extract the 'so-what' very quickly without having to draft tedious data maps. Some of you may find this an inadequate way of looking at your life and that is why there are three other templates available.

Build your happiness framework

Writing this part of the book has been particularly challenging – I researched more than twenty thousand pages and there are tonnes of questionnaires available out there which can measure happiness. Notable among them are: Oxford Happiness Inventory (Argyle and Hill), Subjective Happiness Scale (Lyubomirsky & Lepper), Satisfaction with Life Scale (Deiner, Emmons, Larsen and Griffin) and Panas Scale (Watson, Clark, Tellegen). These questionnaires have been designed by sociologists, psychologists, economists and sometimes multi-disciplinary researchers working collaboratively. They are very well thought through and scientifically designed - the only problem is that they are very difficult to use and have the same scale for all people taking the questionnaire. It is like measuring a unidimensional metric like your height or weight. Is happiness that simple to measure? Can you put a number to your state of mind by just filling a questionnaire? Did we not say that each one of us is a different human being – shaped by millions of interactions through the course of our lives, by the hundreds or thousands of people who have crossed our lives, by the victories and defeats, aspirations and limitations. Resultantly, each of us value different things differently and happiness triggers may differ starkly from one person to the other. Then how can a single scale accommodate an area that has so many dimensions to it – you may be happy with your family but extremely dissatisfied with your professional life.

So let us try to build a simple model that works for all of us – this will become our Happiness Framework. To build this let us take a comprehensive list of factors important for all of us in our lives:

a. Health
b. Relationships
c. Career/Profession
d. Wealth
e. Sex
f. Hobbies/Recreation
g. Spirituality
h. Others

As you can see from the list this is not prescriptive but invites you to include aspects that are important for you in life. Let us talk about each one of them to understand which area drives happiness in what way and then we will get to the model that will help you calculate your happiness score at a specific point in time.

a. Health

The World Health Organization (WHO) defined human health in a broader sense in its 1948 constitution as "a state of complete physical, mental and social well-being and not merely the absence of disease or infirmity." This definition focuses not only on a healthy body but also mental and social well being. Given the large scope of this definition and the difficulty in quantifying this for people the WHO was criticized for creating a goal that was almost impossible to measure and achieve. In 1984, the WHO revised the definition of health to "the extent to which an individual or group is able to realize aspirations and satisfy needs and to change or cope with the environment. Health is a resource for everyday life, not the objective of living; it is a positive concept, emphasizing social and personal resources, as well as physical capacities." This definition also does not limit itself to the physical body alone – it emphasizes the

physical body as a resource for living life to the fullest –
for being able to cope with the changes in environment,
physical and mental challenges and create a harmonious
relationship with society in general.

The Roman poet Juvenal wrote in Satire X (10.356)

" orandum est ut sit mens sana in corpore sano.
    fortem posce animum mortis terrore carentem,
    qui spatium vitae extremum inter munera ponat
    naturae, qui ferre queat quoscumque labores,
    nesciat irasci, cupiat nihil et potiores
    Herculis aerumnas credat saevosque labores
    et venere et cenis et pluma Sardanapalli.
    monstro quod ipse tibi possis dare; semita certe
    tranquillae per virtutem patet unica vitae."

Which translates in English to

"You should pray for a healthy mind in a healthy
body.
    Ask for a stout heart that has no fear of death,
    and deems length of days the least of Nature's gifts
    that can endure any kind of toil,
    that knows neither wrath nor desire and thinks
    the woes and hard labors of Hercules better than
    the loves and banquets and downy cushions of
Sardanapalus.
    What I commend to you, you can give to yourself;
    For assuredly, the only road to a life of peace is
virtue"

Juvenal indicated the first thing to ask God is a healthy
body and mind and this forms the most basic and relevant
definitions of health. Going by 'Mens sana in corpore
sano' meaning 'a healthy mind rests in a healthy body,'

we will focus on the two core components of health: body and mind.

A healthy body is devoid of disease and has the immunity to fight against most infections and diseases, has enough strength to allow for an enjoyable life experience with unconstrained mobility and the ability to uninhibitedly enjoy the various activities that a person may like to pursue. A healthy body not only contributes to a more active, productive and fulfilling life, but can add years to your life. Following some basic guidelines can ensure you develop and maintain a healthy body:

- Balanced diet: A balanced diet is one that gives your body the nutrients it needs to function correctly. Each of us has a different lifestyle and live in different parts of the world with varying climate and occupation. This means that our diet has to be unique to our way of life. The basic principle to adhere to is to have our energy needs covered with naturally occurring major blocks of nutritional foods like proteins, carbohydrates, fat, vitamins and minerals and water. When you eat right, you not only feel better and have more energy, but you also provide your body with vital nutrients that maintain your body's health. A nutrient-rich diet includes whole grains, fish, nuts, eggs, poultry and lean meats, fat-free or low-fat dairy foods such as yogurt and fortified milk, and unsaturated fats like olive oil and avocados. Avoid processed and refined foods, which are typically loaded with saturated fats and sugar. These foods have little nutritional value and can cause your blood glucose levels to rise and then quickly drop, leaving you feeling tired. The intent in this book is to not provide dietary advice but to indicate the importance of a healthy diet as a way to maintain a healthy body and improve happiness levels in life

- Physical activity: Regular physical activity helps control your weight, strengthens your bones and muscles, improves your mood and overall mental health and may add extra years to your life. Physical exercise also leads our bodies to release a chemical called endorphin which is the 'feel good' chemical. You've heard people talk about "runner's high," the feeling of bliss and oneness with the world that comes after running a while. Endorphins are the likely reason why, although some researchers believe other brain chemicals, like serotonin and dopamine, play a role too. Plus, endorphins help to relieve pain. Once you start pumping out endorphins, exercise no longer feels as hard. Finally, endorphins help to calm fear and anxiety, thereby making you feel more tranquil and at peace with yourself. No wonder studies show exercise helps to boost self-esteem and sense of well-being

- Adequate sleep: Sleep is necessary for the healing and repair of your heart and blood vessels. It aids in the balance of your body's hormones and supports your body's growth and development. Your immune system, which defends your body against infections and other harmful substances, relies on adequate sleep to remain strong and function properly. According to the National Sleep Foundation most adults needs seven to nine hours of sleep a night in order for the body and mind to function optimally. But a CDC survey found that more than a third of adults reported less than seven hours of sleep during a typical 24-hour period. Other experts believe the numbers are even more alarming. "Some of the latest polls show that nearly three quarters of the adult population is not getting the recommended amount of sleep," says James Maas, PhD, former chair of the psychology department at Cornell University and author of Sleep for Success. Lack of sleep can lead to increased chances of sickness, weight gain due to hormonal changes and cognitive changes that make it difficult to resist food and poor concentration, memory and decision making when at work, study or play. With an invasion of technology in our bedrooms, sleep has become the sacrificial lamb. Smartphones, tablets and other devices are mentally stimulating and the light from these devices suppresses melatonin a sleep inducing chemical that delays the process of falling asleep. Further, we start to correlate in our minds the bedroom as a place of using gadgets to socialize, play games and have fun but not a place to relax and fall asleep. There is a lot of information out there on how to sleep well which I will not talk about in this book – but one thing is clear – approximately 8 hours of good quality sleep a day is crucial for adults to be able to maintain good health.

We have spoken briefly about the importance of a healthy body and now lets talk about mental health. According to the U.K. surgeon general (1999), mental health is the successful performance of mental function, resulting in productive activities, fulfilling relationships with other people, and providing the ability to adapt to change and cope with adversity. The term mental illness refers collectively to all diagnosable mental disorders—health conditions characterized by alterations in thinking, mood, or behavior associated with distress or impaired functioning. Good mental health isn't just the absence of mental health problems. Being mentally or emotionally healthy is much more than being free of depression, anxiety, or other psychological issues. Rather than the absence of mental illness, mental health refers to the presence of positive characteristics. Mentally healthy people have high self-esteem and self-confidence, a sense of contentment, a zest for living and the ability to bounce back from distress and the ability to develop and maintain fulfilling relationships. Mental health issues are more difficult to diagnose and in some cultures, they are perceived as a sign of weakness or an imaginary issue. Following things can be practiced to develop and maintain good mental health:

- Build self esteem: Value yourself and appreciate the positive traits that you have. Each one of us is blessed with many positive traits which we should use to build self-esteem. Being overly self-critical should be avoided and you should treat yourself with kindness and respect.

- Build positive relations in the real world: Find people who value you for what you are and make you feel good about yourself without giving you a false picture. Build strong social connections with family, friends, support groups, peers, coworkers or other interest groups. Don't focus too much on having too many connections on social media with limited interactions and hardly any genuine relationship. Build a network of people who you can reach out to for support when you need it and offer support to them when they need it in a perfectly symbiotic relationship.

- Practice mindfulness: Different mindfulness techniques work for different people – some like to pray, others like to meditate or do relaxation exercises like Yoga or Tai-Chi. Research shows that mindfulness calms the mind, reduces the impact of uncomforting mental impulses and improves the overall outlook towards life. Mindfulness is both a science and an art and comes with practice. Certain cultures and religions are big on mindfulness and lots can be learnt from Buddhism and Hinduism and associated psycho-physical techniques of Yoga, Tai-chi etc

b. Relationships

Aristotle the legendary Greek philosopher said, "Man is by nature a social animal; an individual who is unsocial naturally and not accidentally is either beneath our notice or more than human. Society is something that precedes the individual."

Man cannot live alone – dependence on society starts with the umbilical bond with the mother and extends until the last breath.

"Society friendship and love/Divinely bestow'd upon man," sang William Cowper, portraying the pangs of solitude of Alexander Selkirk who had been marooned on an uninhabited island for years.

There are practical benefits of healthy relations:

- Increased longevity: A review of 148 studies found that people with strong social relationships are 50% less likely to die prematurely. Similarly, Dan Buettner's Blue Zones research calculates that committing to a life partner can add 3 years to life expectancy (Researchers Nicholas Christakis and James Fowler have found that men's life expectancy benefits from marriage more than women's do.)

- Less stress: In a study of over 100 people, researchers found that people who completed a stressful task experienced a faster recovery when they were reminded of people with whom they had strong relationships. (Those who were reminded of stressful relationships, on the other hand, experienced even more stress and higher blood pressure.)

- Better health and wellbeing: According to research by psychologist Sheldon Cohen, college students who reported having strong relationships were half as likely to catch a common cold when exposed to the virus, while an AARP study with older adults found that loneliness is a significant predictor of poor health. More generally, a 2012 international Gallup poll found that people who feel they have friends and family to count on are generally more satisfied with their personal health than people who feel isolated.

According to psychiatrists Jacqueline Olds and Richard Schwartz, social alienation is an inevitable result of contemporary society's preoccupation with materialism and frantic "busy-ness." Their decades of research supports the idea that a lack of relationships can cause multiple problems with physical, emotional, and spiritual health. The research is clear and devastating: isolation is fatal.

Given the high importance of relationships, let us now look at what are the major types of relationships:

- Friendship: Family is what we get – friends on the other hand, we choose. In this selection process, we tend to have friendships with people who contribute positively to our happiness and wellbeing. Research shows that it is not just important to have friends, the depth and quality of those friendships are also very important. We often enjoy our time with friends more than family since most of that time is spent doing leisurely activities which are largely enjoyable. On the other hand, with family we have to also do things which we don't enjoy too much like attending a wedding or socializing with another family with whom you may not be friends with but have to be polite and find ways to get through that interaction. Acquaintances go through an initial selection process and only then do they become friends. When this selection process is continued throughout a large duration in our life (say 30-40 years) we end up with friends who have stood the test of time and have consistently made us happy. Through these long years the superficial friendships tend to fade away. With friends there are no inhibitions on what can be shared or not, there is little chance to be judged and we are at ease in sharing our biggest fears, secrets, joys or sorrows. This mutual sharing of emotions and the unconditional love and support is what makes friendship special. This is a tremendous contributor to happiness and longevity in life

- Family: Family is your brethren with strong blood links. Family is where your life begins – the first set of people who accept you for what you are with no selection process in place. They are the first sources of unconditional love, support, protection, nutrition, care, education and physical and psychological development. You inherit a lot of things that shape you when you are born thanks to DNA. Family stays with you during good and difficult times – many other relationships crumble when facing the test of difficult times. Imagine how many so called 'friends' you lose when you get fired from your job or are removed from a position of power. Family also forgives you when you commit mistakes and teaches you how not to repeat those mistakes. Other superficial relations do not bother to correct faulty behavior. When children are brought up in happy supportive families they have a solid foundation for life and grow up to be capable adults. There is also tremendous negative impact on children raised in dysfunctional environments. A 2014 Brazilian study confirmed that there are higher incidences of mental health problems in children from dysfunctional families. Children from dysfunctional families often report higher anxiety levels as they inherit higher levels from their parents and are also not allowed the chance to experiment in different life situations in a safe environment where they can succeed or fail without consequences. Children from dysfunctional families have difficulty forging and maintaining strong intimate relationships with people and trusting others. They also have difficulty trusting reality since they may have been given a warped interpretation of reality growing up that their sense of reality is confused. They may have been given wrong statements to manipulate their sense of reality and to create a make-believe world. While nobody can choose what kind of a family you are born in but there are steps that can be taken to enhance the positive impact of a loving and caring family and also of minimizing the damage from a dysfunctional family.

- Romantic: The Beatles sang "I need somebody to love" and they were so right – we all need a strong connection with that someone special who can keep us happy and satisfied. Harry Reis in the Encyclopedia of Human Relationships states that there is very nice evidence that people who engage in long term stable and satisfying romantic relationships fare better on a variety of health measures. The vicissitudes of a romance initially can be a source of stress and may not bring immediate health benefits. People in healthy stable relationships take better care of themselves – your spouse may remind you of healthy eating habits or may discourage you from alcohol or substance abuse. Over time these healthy habits lead to fewer illnesses. Happily married couples report lowered blood pressure – on the other end of the spectrum unhappy couples report heightened blood pressure worse than single people. Quality of marriage matters more than being married or not. Happily married couples report lowered anxiety, less bodily pains and aches, better stress management, faster healing from diseases and wounds and a longer happier life.

- Professional: We spend a very large part of our lives with professional contacts. Workplace relationships can enrich employees' experiences at work by satisfying their psychological needs for affiliation. Employees who struggle to form personal relationships with co-workers can find their morale decreasing on the job, and they may be more likely to leave a job than employees who look forward to seeing friends each day. Work life does not always deliver positive experiences, and employees may find themselves needing others to support them during stressful or discouraging times on the job. Employees who form personal relationships at work are more likely to rebound quickly from things such as negative performance reviews or gossip around the office. By the same token, it is also nice to have people on your side to celebrate work-related victories, such as promotions and pay raises. Workplace accomplishments can turn into memorable experiences with a group of friends at your side. Even birthdays spent at work can become memorable occasions with good friends by your side.

c. Career/Profession

Abrahim Lincoln said "Whatever you are, be a good one." Most of us spend the first quarter of our lives acquiring the skills needed in a field of choice so that we can pursue a profession and build a career out of this pursuit. This career provides us with not just a primary source of income but also a sense of purpose and achievement. An area where we impart our acquired knowledge and help create value for society. Over a period we begin to be known based on our career – John is a Doctor, Jack is a firefighter and so on. This becomes our primary identity in society and our primary contribution to society. It also becomes the most common arena for competition amongst peers – most students from Business schools aspire to become CEOs and commonly gauge relative success by comparing where they are with where their fellow students have reached. Success in career directly impacts financial status, social status, self-worth, self-image and your ability to create better conditions and opportunities for your family. Success provides confidence, security, a sense of well-being, the ability to contribute at a greater level, hope and leadership. Without success, you, the group, your company, your goals, dreams and even entire civilizations cease to survive. Darwinian evolutionary theory also ensures that we all keep striving to be successful and fuel further innovation and betterment for society by trying to be better than the rest.

For many people this becomes the primary and most important goal in life for a large part of life. No wonder "I am slammed" or "I work too much" is a completely acceptable phrase among professionals in high paying careers trying to climb the quintessential corporate ladder. This becomes a way of saying "I am elite and I am important" – a subtle way of showing your superiority. Not only is working hard a way of enacting status it is also a display of heroism or machismo. Working long hours is seen as a "heroic activity," noted Cynthia Fuchs Epstein and her co-authors in their 1999 study of lawyers.

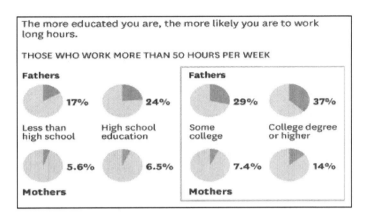

The more educated you are, the more likely you are to work long hours.

THOSE WHO WORK MORE THAN 50 HOURS PER WEEK

Fathers
17% — Less than high school
24% — High school education

5.6% — 6.5%
Mothers

Fathers
29% — Some college
37% — College degree or higher

7.4% — 14%
Mothers

Source: US census bureau 2011

Media today is full of Machiavellian idolization of corporate CEOs – giving them almost God like status. Everything they do – right from the way they dress, to their philanthropic activities to daily schedules and reading habits - is studied and broadcasted to millions of people via various media channels. There is a multibillion industry on studying leadership styles and guiding wannabe leaders on how to become one. This 'God like' status given to modern day CEOs by the media creates a cult like infatuation. People see these leaders as the personification of their own aspirations, dreams, goals, hopes and desires. Consequently, many people aspire to become like their heroes and spend a very large amount of time in trying to achieve success in their careers. The definition of success being the attainment of the 'CEO' or a senior management position in a large company. According to the OECD, Mexico and Costa Rica have the longest working hours in the world at over 2200 hours annually.

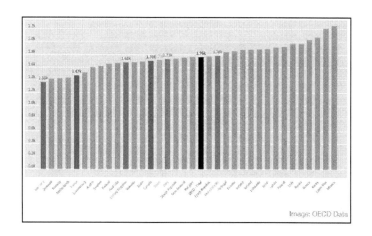

Image: OECD Data

This does not, unfortunately, translate into Mexicans or Costa Ricans being the most successful people in the world – only 1 Mexican is in the list of the top 10 richest people in the world and none of the Fortune 10 companies has a Mexican or Costa Rican CEO. This shows there is no direct correlation between long working hours and corporate or financial success.

No. ≑	Name ≑	Net worth (USD) (March 2018) ≑	Age ≑	Nationality ≑	Source(s) of wealth ≑
1 ▲	Jeff Bezos	$112.0 billion ▲	54	United States	Amazon
2 ▼	Bill Gates	$90.0 billion ▲	62	United States	Microsoft
3 ▼	Warren Buffett	$84.0 billion ▲	87	United States	Berkshire Hathaway
4 ▲	Bernard Arnault	$72.0 billion ▲	69	France	LVMH
5 –	Mark Zuckerberg	$71.0 billion ▲	33	United States	Facebook
6 ▼	Amancio Ortega	$70.0 billion ▼	81	Spain	Inditex, Zara
7 ▼	Carlos Slim	$67.1 billion ▲	78	Mexico	América Móvil, Grupo Carso
8 –	Charles Koch	$60.0 billion ▲	82	United States	Koch Industries
8 –	David Koch	$60.0 billion ▲	77	United States	Koch Industries
10 ▼	Larry Ellison	$58.5 billion ▲	73	United States	Oracle Corporation

There is, however, strong evidence that long working hours have an adverse effect on your health and productivity. Working a 55-hour week brings with it a risk of coronary heart disease and stroke, says a recent research article published in The Lancet. Working long hours can also make you fatter, increase your risk of diabetes and make you depressed. It can even lead to an early death. A study looking at the health of people who sat for a long time found that they had a nearly 50% increased risk of death from any cause. Clearly, working long hours does not make you healthy; let us now see how it affects productivity in the workplace. According to Stanford's John Pencavel, productivity drops dramatically with long hours. In one case employees who worked hard for an additional 14 hours produced nothing more – absolute zilch. In economic terms, the employee actually costed the company more money by staying longer and produced no value for this additional time. Therefore, long working hours may infact be detrimental for companies – a stark contrast to many companies where 90hr weeks are celebrated. Some companies have started to reward employees attaining good work-life balance; Aetna the American insurance company has introduced a sleep scheme – every employee sleeping longer than 7 hours for 20 nights gets a $25 reward.

Clearly, the importance of a successful career varies by person and each one of us has a different way of going about and achieving our goals. Therefore, how happy or unhappy it makes you also varies by person. More on this when we get to the Happiness Index.

d. Wealth (Financial security)

"There is something about poverty that smells like death" – Zora Neale Hurston.

Money or the equivalent in resources is the most basic need of any human. It is needed to acquire food, water, shelter, sense of security, education and almost everything in life. Abject poverty on the other hand limits nutrition, access to education, sanitation, healthcare, and almost all other things needed to live a contend and enjoyable life. There is strong scientific evidence of the correlation of wealth and happiness in life – in a psychological study of 4000 millionaires from 17 countries – higher levels of wealth were linked to greater well-being. Another interesting finding is that how this money was earned also has an impact on happiness – self earned money leads to more happiness than acquired wealth. Researchers believe that wealth might increase happiness by providing a greater sense of autonomy. The more wealth a person has, the more freedom they have to choose how to spend their time. As people pursue activities that they like this directly improves their happiness levels. These activities also enable further social connections with new people some of whom may become friends over a period of time and after due voluntary or involuntary selection. With money, people may also acquire objects which give them a higher social status and lead to improved self-image and heightened self-esteem. A good example is buying an expensive sports car – while it gives an immediate increase in self-esteem it also enables the owner to indulge in more happiness enhancing experiences like long drives and more social outings to exhibit his or her new purchase. It should be noted however that just the purchase of the car may lead to a bump in happiness levels in the short term but in the long term just the purchase will not lead to increased happiness – it is how this acquired object is used to collect experiences which determines the long term contribution to happiness. Money also acts as a safety net – investments done by parents help secure the future of their children, give certainty on higher education; in case of serious diseases having enough money means access to high quality medical care which may be the difference between life and death. This safety net shields people from the stress that many situations that life throws at you – having enough money can often be the key to finding solutions to these complex situations and can greatly reduce related stress and anxiety leading to increased happiness levels.

Researchers found that money contributes to happiness to meet basic needs -- but above a certain level, more money does not yield much more happiness. Happiness levels do not increase much beyond USD 75000 because increases beyond this level do not improve quality of life by that much.

There are also differences in how men and women think about money. Men are raised to see the world as hierarchical and competitive. There's always a one-up and one-down position, a winner and a loser. Women see the world as cooperative and democratic; they share. In addition, they are allowed--even encouraged--to be needy and vulnerable, while men are discouraged from such display. Despite many social changes, men are still bred to believe they will be good at dealing with money-- although nobody tells them how to do it. In that way, money is like sex; they're just supposed to know. Women are raised to believe they won't be good at it. When men make money in the stock market, they credit their own cleverness. When they lose money, they blame the incompetence of their advisors or bad luck. When women make money in the market, they credit the cleverness of their advisors, good luck or even the stars. When they lose money, they blame themselves. Men are trained to believe that money equals power and that power is the path to respect. Another important difference between men and women concerns their interests in merging their money. Typically, men want to merge all the couple money--while maintaining primary decision-making power. Women want to keep at least some money separate. Clearly, money can be a big source of happiness or the reason for a lot of dissatisfaction with life.

"Money isn't everything ... but it ranks right up there with oxygen." – Zig Ziglar

e. Sex

"We waste time looking for the perfect lover, instead of creating the perfect love." — Tom Robbins

The University of Canterbury in New Zealand asked 173 people to rate things they did each day and how pleasurable, meaningful, and happy each made them feel. Sex came out on top followed by drinking and partying, and then down the list came volunteering, religious activities, and playing with children. Top negative ranking activities in terms of happiness quotients included getting over an illness and texting. The physical and emotional act of having sex has multiple benefits. Sex causes increased production of oxytocin, which is often referred to as the "love hormone". Before orgasm, oxytocin, released from the brain, surges and is accompanied by the release of endorphins, our natural pain-killing hormones. The endorphins released during sexual intercourse and orgasms are natural mood-boosters and stress relievers. Regular sex can also boost your self-esteem and increase intimacy between partners.

For those in a monogamous relationship, studies have found that semen does contain several mood-altering hormones that can reduce depression and elevated mood. Intercourse, depending on your level of enthusiasm, can be considered aerobic exercise, burning up to 200 calories per session. Among other benefits, women who engage in regular sexual activity with their partners have higher levels of estrogen, which protects against heart disease. Research has found that men who have sex two times per week have fewer heart attacks than those who do not. Women who have more sex have higher levels of estrogen, which is essential to enjoying healthier, smoother skin. It also promotes the production of collagen, which keeps the skin supple and gives you a healthy glow.

The other question is – does it matter who you have sex with? Is it just the physical act of sex that makes people happy? According to stats from happify.com 96% people reported sex being more fulfilling when there is an emotional connection between partners. It is also scientifically proven that married people or people in stable long term relationships have sex more frequently – for people between ages 25 and 59 – 25% of married people have sex 2-3 times per week while less than 5% of single people have sex that frequently. Further, couples who cuddle up after sex report higher levels of happiness that the ones who don't.

What about infidelity? What happens when you have emotional and/or physical digressions with people other than your spouse? What are the effects of breaking the assumed and often religious contract of sexual and emotional exclusivity? We are living in an age where income levels are the highest, everything can be accessed with a single click, our liabilities and limitations are at an all time low, we have access to all kinds of knowledge, materials and knowhow over the internet, there are multiple communication channels – public and covert where all kinds of desires can be tried and experienced. This makes infidelity or cheating easier to access and with a lowered probability of being caught. People cheat for different reasons – emotional void in current relationship, sexual desires not being fulfilled, the thrill of tasting the forbidden fruit, an escape from the humdrum of routine and many other reasons. According to The New York Times, the most consistent data on infidelity comes from the University of Chicago's General Social Survey (GSS). Interviews with people in non-monogamous relationships since 1972 by the GSS have shown that approximately 12% of men and 7% of women admit to having had an extramarital relationship. Results, however, vary year by year, and also by age-group surveyed. For example, one study conducted by the University of Washington, Seattle found slightly, or significantly higher rates of infidelity for populations under 35, or older than 60. In that study which involved 19,065 people during a 15-year period, rates of infidelity among men were found to have risen from 20 to 28%, and rates for women, 5% to 15%.

Why is infidelity so common? Our evolutionary cousins may offer some genetic clues which id like to explore to understand this better. Apes are our closest living relatives. There are only a handful of species, but they show great diversity in their mating systems. Gibbons are monogamous, pairing for life barring the occasional infidelity. Chimpanzees live in multi-male and multi-female communities, promiscuously mating with each other. Gorillas live in polygynous groups in which several females are dominated by a single male. In the animal kingdom, monogamy in the strictest sense of sexual exclusivity is largely a myth. Where it does occur, the factors underpinning it are either coldly pragmatic, or bloodcurdling.

Our natural instinct is to be polygamous – but humanity has developed a moral code – a rulebook of sorts for society - over the past centuries and this is a significant departure from our basic primitive animalistic instincts in many ways. One notable example is monogamy – the explicit contract backed by religious, social and political authorities to be sexually and emotionally loyal to one partner. The practice of this social code over centuries has deeply ingrained in our minds that infidelity is immoral, anti-social even criminal. Consequently, any act of infidelity causes tremendous guilt and the inability to share it with anybody close to you further leaves you alone handling a major crisis with no support system at your disposal. I do not at all preach or support infidelity but if the impending guilt can be avoided then the act itself will not create havoc in your mind. How it plays out with your partner is a completely different topic but of equal if not more importance. I'm no relationship counselor and therefore will refrain from providing relationship advice but the same sense of betrayal will have to be minimized for the partner to be able to accept this. Even in the modern world there are successful polygamous relationships in the Arab and African cultures which are well accepted by society and do not cause conflict or other issues. There are multiple models that work for different people depending upon their religious beliefs and the culture that they have been brought up in. Ultimately, what becomes most important is the way our sexual behavior is in tune with our personal values and beliefs.

f.   Hobbies/Recreation

"You never lose a dream, it just incubates as a hobby" – Larry Page

I asked a colleague recently – what do you do in your free time? He looked surprised and retorted – "I work 70 hours a week and I have three kids, between work and family life goes by without me getting the time to pursue a hobby – I barely get to watch news headlines on TV." The conversation then rambled on to how glorious the onset of spring is going to be this year and how he enjoys tending to his small garden on weekends. I asked him if he enjoys spending time in his garden so much isn't that a hobby – he said yes but I don't do anything fancy and this is not something he is proud to share with his far more adventurous colleagues with fancier hobbies like paragliding, scuba diving or researching renaissance era art.

A hobby is something you do for yourself, it is fun and brings you a lot of pleasure and makes you feel good. There is nothing too trivial to not classify to be a hobby. But why are hobbies important? Hobbies help us create a clear divide between our duties towards others and what we do very selfishly for ourselves. When you lose yourself doing something and are fully immersed in it so much so that time passes by without noticing it is called 'flow' – a term coined by Hungarian-American psychologist Mihaly Csikszentmihalyi. 'Flow' is a state of concentration or complete absorption with the activity at hand and the situation. It is a state in which people are so involved in an activity that nothing else seems to matter. The idea of flow is identical to the feeling of being in the zone or in the groove. The flow state is an optimal state of intrinsic motivation, where the person is fully immersed in what they are doing. This is a feeling everyone has at times, characterized by a feeling of great absorption, engagement, fulfillment, and skill—and during which temporal concerns (time, food, ego-self, etc.) are typically ignored. Mental state in terms of challenge level and skill level, according to Csikszentmihalyi's flow model are depicted below.

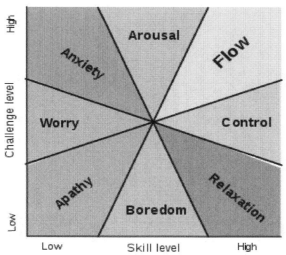

The pursuit of hobbies benefits us in many ways:

- Sense of accomplishment: Hobbies allow us to pursue an activity where we set a goal and then work relentlessly towards achieving the goal. For example for painters the goal is to finish a painting, for stamp collectors the goal is to complete a collection and the list can go on. The achievement of these goals gives us the much-needed feeling of accomplishment and success and this leads to the release of the chemical dopamine – the 'feel good' chemical. This can be especially useful when we don't have much success in other realms of life. This makes us feel like a winner and provides the positivity needed to pursue a fulfilling and healthy life

- Positive engagement: The pursuit of hobbies keeps us engaged in our free time in activities that bring us joy and satisfaction. Since we are engaged in positive activities we refrain from negative behaviors like consumption of alcohol or substance abuse, depressive thoughts and tendencies and other wasteful activities

- Gateway to socializing: Hobbies often involve group activities and this leads to socializing with new people. This helps meeting people with common interests who may be from different age groups and different occupations and different situation in life. This helps broadening your view of the world and taking your own situation in the right perspective. Many a times best friendships are formed when like minded people do things that they love together. Natural barriers are lowered and with high levels of dopamine it becomes easy to make new friends. We have discussed earlier how it is beneficial to have genuine friends with whom most of life's sorrows, problems and joys can be shared

- Discovering hidden talents: Pursuing hobbies gives us a passage to discover our own hidden talents, talents that always existed but never surfaced since the platform to use them never arose. The story of Kentucky Fried Chicken founder, a successful US fast food chain, Harlan David Sanders stands out – Colonel Sanders loved cooking all his life as a hobby but founded the company after he turned 65 years old. He was never a professional chef and did different jobs all his life like insurance agent, steamboat pilot and a farmer. When he hit forty, he opened a service station and starting selling chicken dinners to his customers--developing his pressure frying method over a number of years. Interstate 75 was constructed and it took away all his business but that's when he came up with the idea of franchising and the rest is history as they say

- Love finder: There are many love at first sight stories which happen with the backdrop of both partners pursuing something that they love together. On dating sites most people search for partners based on physical appearance and common interests and hobbies among other factors. In fact there are sites like LoveFlutter where people are matched to each other solely based on common interests. Relationship experts predict that relationships are stronger when both partners can respect each other's hobbies and interests

g. Spirituality

"Just as a candle cannot burn without fire, men cannot live without a spiritual life" – Buddha

Spirituality is difficult to narrow down to a single definition. Scholarly research conducted on the topic led to 27 different definitions most of them very different from each other. I will share what I think it means to me; you should define it for yourself though. I think of spirituality as the connection between a man and a higher belief system that acts as a guide when you face various situations in life where a fully rational decision is difficult to make. There are two elements here – a belief system and a conduit to it. Different religions around the world have tried to provide to us these two elements - a God(s) as a belief system and religious practices that encompass a wide array of activities as the conduit. This has often led to spirituality being confused with the practice of a specific religion.

Why is spirituality important?

For us to function well, our mind, body and spirit have to be in harmony with each other. It is only then that we can lead a healthy fulfilling life where we are able to contribute positively to society. Spiritual health therefore becomes the fine balance that accentuates our well being.

How can we practice spirituality?

Waaijman, in his study on spirituality, mentions four forms of spiritual practice:

- Psychological practices: Meditation
- Social practices: Being part of a larger group, contributing to it by participating in collective events/occasions, contributing to common causes like fundraisers, charity events
- Mindfulness practices: Praying, chanting, meditating are all examples of mindfulness practices
- Somatic practices: Practices like fasting also are a kind of spiritual practice

How does spirituality benefit us?

Research from the Oregon State University shows a connection between your beliefs and your sense of well being. Positive beliefs, comfort, and strength gained from religion, meditation, and prayer can contribute to well being. It may even promote healing. Improving your spiritual health may not cure an illness, but it may help you feel better. It also may prevent some health problems and help you cope better with illness, stress, or death. Practicing spirituality helps reduce stress – in a study of 1300 adults meditation decreased stress levels; the effect was strongest in individuals with the highest levels of stress. An eight-week study of mindfulness meditation helped participants reduce their anxiety. It also reduced symptoms of anxiety disorders, such as phobias, social anxiety, paranoid thoughts, obsessive-compulsive behaviors and panic attacks. Meditation may also help control job-related anxiety in high-pressure work environments. One study found that a meditation program reduced anxiety in a group of nurses. Inflammatory chemicals called cytokines, which are released in response to stress, can affect mood, leading to depression. A review of several studies suggests meditation may reduce depression by decreasing these inflammatory chemicals. Some forms of meditation may help you develop a stronger understanding of yourself, helping you grow into your best self. For example, self-inquiry meditation explicitly aims to help you develop a greater understanding of yourself and how you relate to those around you. Other forms teach you to recognize thoughts that may be harmful or self-defeating. The idea is that as you gain greater awareness of your thought habits, you can steer them toward more constructive patterns. Focused-attention meditation is like weight lifting for your attention span. It helps increase the strength and endurance of your attention. For example, a study looked at the effects of an eight-week mindfulness meditation course and found it improved participants' ability to reorient and maintain their attention. The mental discipline you can develop through meditation may help you break dependencies by increasing your self-control and awareness of triggers for addictive behaviors. One study that taught 19 recovering alcoholics how to meditate found that participants who received the training got better at controlling their cravings and craving-related stress. One study compared two mindfulness-based meditation programs by randomly assigning participants to one of two groups. One group practiced meditation, while the other didn't. Participants who meditated fell asleep sooner and stayed asleep longer, compared to those who didn't meditate. Meditation can also improve physical health by reducing strain on the heart. Over time, high blood pressure makes the heart work harder to pump blood, which can lead to poor heart function. High blood pressure also contributes to atherosclerosis, or narrowing of the arteries, which can lead to heart attacks and strokes. A study of 996 volunteers found that when they meditated by concentrating on a "silent mantra" — a repeated, non-vocalized word — reduced blood pressure by about five points, on average. This was more effective among older volunteers and those who had higher blood pressure prior to the study

Religious practices usually prescribe a healthy lifestyle – refraining from consumption of alcohol and tobacco, occasional fasting, healthy eating habits etc When these healthy practices are combined with spiritual practices the benefits to overall wellbeing are profound.

h. Others

There are many other drivers of happiness which together for me constituted an individual category - others. Each one of these can be very important to many of you and this list can in no way be comprehensive. Think of it as a collection of thoughts and ideas on various drivers of happiness.

- Start giving: Winston Churchill once aptly stated – "We make a living by what we get. We make a life by what we give". Humans are trained to compete and win – leaving behind others and coming first which triggers satisfaction of achieving your goals. Society doesn't brand you 'successful' if you don't come first, conversely, leave the rest behind. Billions of dollars are poured into making people learn how to come first be it in education, business, sports, showbiz or any other walk of life. At the same time, we feel sorry for people who 'have been left behind'. The sight of poor, homeless people who cant afford two square meals a day breaks our heart. We often blame the system, governments, politicians, bureaucracy, capitalism – anything that is far from our control. We blame the unknown shirking off responsibility for whats around us – and its true that we may not have directly caused the misery but it is also true that each one of us can do our bit to reduce it. Researchers from the University of Zurich in Switzerland told 50 people they'd be receiving about $100 over a few weeks. Half of the people were asked to commit to spending that money on themselves, and half were asked to spend it on someone they knew. The researchers wanted to see whether simply pledging to being generous was enough to make people happier. So before doling out any money, they brought everyone into the lab and asked them to think about a friend they'd like to give a gift to and how much they would hypothetically spend. They then performed functional MRI scans to measure activity in three regions of the brain associated with social behavior, generosity, happiness and decision-making. Their choices—and their brain activity—seemed to depend on how they had pledged to spend the money earlier. Those who had agreed to spend money on other people tended to make more generous decisions throughout the experiment, compared to those who had agreed to spend on themselves. They also had more interaction between the parts of the brain associated with altruism and happiness, and they reported higher levels of happiness after the experiment was over. Another piece of good news was that it didn't seem to matter how generous people were. Planning to give away just a little bit of money had the same effects on happiness as giving away a lot. "At least in our study, the amount spent did not matter," said lead author Philippe Tobler, associate professor of neuroeconomics and social neuroscience, in an email. "It is worth keeping in mind that even little things have a beneficial effect—like bringing coffee to one's office mates in the morning."

I personally believe that just giving money away is the first convenient step– the bigger step to take is to participate in the project that your money funds. Imagine being able to feel the impact of your contribution first hand. If you are really keen to improve something in thi world – go there and help fix it yourself. See the plight with your eyes, put in effort to fix it and see the results with your own eyes. If you want to educate the uneducated, start teaching. If you want to provide shelter to the homeless start by visiting a shelter and see what more needs to be done. The basic message is – start giving, and if possible start participating in activities which you give to. This will bring you a sense of directly helping someone in need and will make you feel better about yourself.

- Practice gratitude: "Gratitude unlocks the fullness of life. It turns what we have into enough." — Melodie Beatty. In our unquenchable thirst for more we forget how lucky we are to have what we have. We take what we have for granted and chase the things we don't have. To be able to value what you have, you have think about it from the perspective of the people who don't have it. Speak to someone who had a rough childhood to realize how lucky you were to have escaped the scars which will stay on with him forever. Imagine the plight of a couple trying to have kids for decades – and realize how lucky you are to have kids.

Imagine what a hot meal means to millions of people around the world who go hungry. Imagine the plight of parents who's child has an incurable disease, no matter what they do, their child will suffer and eventually die. Feeling and expressing gratitude turns our mental focus to the positive, which compensates for our brain's natural tendency to focus on threats, worries, and negative aspects of life. As such, gratitude creates positive emotions, like joy, love, and contentment, which research shows can undo the grip of negative emotions, like anxiety. Fostering gratitude can also broaden your thinking and create positive cycles of thinking and behaving in healthy, positive ways. In a study conducted on the topic, 65 adults with neuromuscular disease were asked either to write gratitude diaries for a 21-day period or to just fill in the assessments of mood, well-being, and health without actually having an intervention (control condition). Those in the gratitude condition also had their partners rate their mood and life satisfaction. Results showed that the gratitude group had more positive views of their life as a whole than control participants. They also reported a more positive mood and less negative mood on a daily basis during the study period. Their partners also reported that the gratitude participants had a more positive mood and greater satisfaction with life. With respect to health, the gratitude condition actually improved participants' sleep — both amount and quality. Perhaps focusing on life's blessings reduced the worry and angst that keep people awake at night.

Researchers from the University of Georgia interviewed couples about how happy they were in their marriage. They found that expressing gratitude was a consistent predictor of happiness. They studied 468 couples, asking them about their communication styles, financial issues, and how often they expressed gratitude. According to the study, couples who were likely to show their appreciation were more likely to power through obstacles that bring a lot of relationships down: money issues, for example. The study's lead author said: "It goes to show the power of 'thank you.' Even if a couple is experiencing distress and difficulty in other areas, gratitude in the relationship can help promote positive marital outcomes." It makes sense. When you're feeling grateful, you're in a better emotional state. You've slowed down to enjoy the moment and be a little more mindful of it. That gives you the breathing room to open yourself up to others and try to understand them a little more.

One way to regularly practice gratitude is to write a gratitude diary – start with a monthly cadence and if this is something that benefits you then increase cadence to weekly or even daily. Many religions around the world include a healthy dose of gratitude in their daily prayer rituals – "thank you God for what you have given us" is a gratitude message to God intended for us to realize the value of all what we have.

- Learn to deal with guilt:

"So full of artless jealousy is guilt,
It spills itself in fearing to be spilt."
— William Shakespeare

Guilt is the result of your actions that do not conform to your self-image. Whenever you do something that is not in line with your value or belief system it makes you feel bad causing negative emotions to trigger. You question am I really this bad? Am I not true to the value system that my loved ones have tried to inculcate in me? Guilt is not necessarily a bad thing if you know how to manage all the complex emotions that come with it. According to the Harvard Business Review people who are prone to guilt tend to work harder and perform better than people who are not guilt-prone, and are perceived to be more capable leaders. People who often feel guilty are better friends, lovers and employees; people who expect to feel guilty tend to be more sympathetic, to put themselves into other people's shoes, to think about the consequences of their behaviour before acting, and to treasure their morals. As a result, they are less prone to lie, cheat or behave immorally when they conduct a business deal or spot an opportunity to make money, studies suggest. They are also likely to make better employees because people who think less about the future results of their actions are more likely to be late, to steal or to be rude to clients. Too much of guilt, though, is not a good thing - self-criticism is consistently associated with less motivation and worse self-control. It is also one of the single biggest predictors of depression.

Not doing anything so you never feel guilty is practically impossible – you will at some point in time skip a diet, not go to the gym, miss a meeting, avoid someone you don't like etc. So feeling guilty is unavoidable. How do we then deal with it? Firstly, it is important to put things into their rightful place in life. Very often things are blown out of proportion to make them look bigger than they are – it is important you set rational limits. Skipping a diet is bad but is it worth pondering over for months? So feeling guilty for stuff in proportion to its importance in life is okay. Secondly, take responsibility for your actions – don't make excuses or blame others. If you were late for a meeting – don't blame traffic – you could have planned better! Owning up to your mistakes makes you feel fully incharge – it also shows people around you that you are responsible and truthful – this further builds trust. Imagine a situation where instead of giving lame excuses to your boss about being late for a project you own up to your shortcomings and promise to not repeat the mistakes and do a better job next time. Your boss will start to think of you differently knowing you are in control, you are honest and you will take the right corrective actions to remedy the situation. Thirdly, cut yourself some slack – we are humans – not machines; we are all imperfect, we are all work in progress. Go easy on yourselves – you are the only constant in your life and you should treat yourselves fairly and with respect. Fourthly, take charge and act - the feeling of guilt should trigger corrective action. For example, if not working out for a week makes you feel guilty then go out and exercise to fix it. Inaction on top of guilt further compounds the feeling of guilt and makes you more miserable. Taking action makes you feel bigger than the problem and shows to you you are in charge and powerful enough to remedy the situation. Lastly, confess, ask for forgiveness and let go when you cannot do anything about what happened in the past. Many times you knowingly or unknowingly do things which do not seem that big when they start but lead to disastrous consequences for you and/or people around you close to you. Road accidents involving others when you were driving fall in this category – you don't want to cause harm but due to the sequence of events and partly less careful driving leading to someone losing their life can have disastrous consequences. Most crimes aren't very well planned and happen due to a momentary lapse of judgement and sudden rage. It is helpful to be able to confess to someone – a friend, family member, God and find an outlet for your bottled up emotions. This helps diffuse the built up emotional pressure – in many cultures it is said sharing sorrow reduces it and sharing happiness increases it. The severity of the deed may warrant a prolonged period of confession and cleansing.

- Avoid social media/tech overload:

"Technology is a useful servant but a dangerous master." - Christian Lous Lange

In the last decade technology has formed an inescapable cocoon around all of us – we are constantly bombarded with emails, social media updates and messages, news updates, sales offers – the list is endless. With our social media contacts spread around the world this stream of messages is 24X7 – endless, constant, ever more irrelevant and increasingly non-value adding. Add to it our FOMO – fear of missing out which leads to our devices being closer to us than anything or anyone else. The first thing we do in the day is to check our phones and the last thing we do before sleeping is to check it. According to Statista, daily social media usage of internet users amounted to 135 minutes a day in 2017 up from 126 minutes in the previous year. 135 minutes!! It is 2 hours and 15 minutes – almost a tenth of your day! And it is usually not at a stretch – it is interspersed throughout the day – there is always something you are thinking about at the back of your mind. Research has suggested that young people who spend more than two hours a day on social networking sites are more likely to report poor mental health. If you're on Instagram, there are examples aplenty of overly-filtered simulations of life that are supposed to be 'aspirational' but instead make many users feel like we're having a worse life than our peers. The constant barrage of messages and updates keeps the mind working and busy – never allowing it to relax and quite simply put get bored. Boredom is like a breather for your brain where you start to think a bit differently, more creatively, more divergent from your normal train of thoughts. Some of the greatest sparks of the mind have taken place during a bored state of mind – Newton's discovery of gravity being a prime example. Without the brain getting a chance to relax our ability to think beyond the here and now is constrained. Constant distractions also lead to an obvious loss of productivity – many employers have banned social media sites in the office for this very reason.

Clearly isolating ourselves from technology in today's world is not possible – there is atleast some cost associated to it. What is needed is self-regulation – setting boundaries for social media and tech usage. I would refrain from prescribing approaches but Google the term and there are suggestions aplenty – ranging from creating dedicated time slots to complete tech detox in a prison like environment in South Korea for overworked and stressed out young executives (Its true!).

"Excessive sorrow laughs, excessive joy weeps" – William Blake

• Reduce clutter and chaos

"Be content with what you have, rejoice in the way things are. When you realize there is nothing lacking, the whole world belongs to you." – Lao Tzu

We carry an amazing amount of junk in our lives – with time passing by we keep acquiring things but not disposing. We start with the small picnic grill, then upgrade to the middle sized charcoal grill, few years later we buy the professional gas grill but keep the old picnic grill just in case we go for a picnic and might need it again. It's the same with tools – you buy the basics, then you buy a garage and you want to fill up that space with more tools – most of which you will never use. Throwing things away doesn't come naturally – after all we have paid for it and 'may' use it sometime in the future. This leads to a net addition of things all of which neither are used regularly nor are they disposed – they just sit – occupying physical and mental space. One in every eleven Americans pays for space to store material overflow from their homes – 2.3 billion square feet of storage space and an industry worth 38 Billion US dollars growing at a whopping 12%! This is also true for people – we carry so many negative, energy-sapping relationships without realizing that collectively they are a drag on your happiness and your life.

Reducing clutter and chaos basically means keeping what's essential and getting rid of the rest. Minimalism is a fashionable name given to this approach of life – but in the spirit of moderation let us not try and be too revolutionary but still get the job done. Lets focus first on things. Let us start by asking the uncomfortable question – do you know what all you have? Most probably not – given you don't know what you have its highly likely you don't know what you should throw. Afterall you cant improve what you cant measure – right? So lets start with an approach – I loved the 90/90 rule from Joshua Fields Millburn and Ryan Nicodemus – the duo behind 'The

137

Minimalists'. Take every item you have in your household and ask yourself 2 questions: 1. Have I used this in the past 90 days? And 2. Will I use it in the next 90 days? If the answer to both your questions is 'No' you can throw that thing away. Start with one room and see the results for yourself. If you want to take drastic measures reduce the time threshold of 90 days to 60 or even 30 days. Go through your clothes, your books, those old CDs, unused appliances, pieces of furniture that have never been used, music system, toys, shoes, old papers – leave nothing untouched. If you feel uncomfortable throwing away things which can be used by someone – donate them to charity or better still try and sell them on ebay – make some money while decluttering. Technology can be a boon – all the songs and films stored on your DVDs/CDs can be transferred to your mobile phone or a storage device or better still can be stored on the cloud. Instead of each house having a lawnmower why not have a shared lawnmower with your neighbors. Rent stuff when you need it – instead of buying it.

We are buying things at an unprecedented rate – our reckless consumption (often for throwing it away without fully using it) is leading to serious environmental consequences. In 2017, August 3rd was the Earth Overshoot Day – a day when humans have used up their allowance of natural resources that mother Earth can replenish in a year. Whatever we consume after that cannot be replenished within a year. The overshot day came earlier in 2017 than it did in 2016 signaling our growing pace of destruction of natural resources.

Humans need 1.7 planets to offset our use of natural resources each year. We can all contribute to slowing our pace on this path of destruction by consuming less and more responsibly. How can we consume less? By buying things that you surely need and will use regularly in the future. For every new item you buy throw away 2 old items – this way your net result will always be favorable. Buy only things you need – we are flooded with discount offers and sales every week – buy what you really need rather than trying to clinch a deal. Ask yourself do you really need those new pair of shoes or that new bag. And be aware that what you are buying has been manufactured thousands of miles away from you – raw materials have been transported thousands of miles to the production site – finished goods will be packaged in plastic, stickers, labels, boxes and then the retailer who you buy it from will further package it to deliver it to your doorstep. Do you really need this product or are you buying it because single click buying makes it irresistibly convenient for you. Not a long time ago we used to repair electrical and electronic goods – not anymore, in this era of consumption on steroids any small fault and the gadget gets replaced! Technology is also advancing at a fast pace leading to shorter product life cycles and the need to replenish/upgrade them earlier than in the past. Reducing consumption is not only good for the environment, it saves you money, it saves you space, allows you to focus on the right things and makes you feel good about yourself.

Just as things create clutter and unwanted stress in your lives so do toxic people. They never make a positive contribution to your life and always seem to pull you into their crises. You being the good natured person you are oblige each time without realizing how that time and energy could have been put to better use. The journey here also starts with identifying who those people are – just go through your contact list from time to time and identify the people who are draining you of your peace of mind. We often expect that these people will change and in this hope do not take the step of eliminating them from our lives. Toxic people are not motivated by what's good for them or for their relationship with you. They're motivated by their own complex problems and needs. When you give up the desire to change them, it's much easier to let them go. Start by setting clear boundaries and limits. Don't take calls at anytime of the day; don't make yourself available for every small thing that goes wrong in their life. Don't let them pull you into every crises - toxic people create drama deliberately in order to attract more attention and engage in manipulation, so remember this the next time you're asked to run to their side. You might feel bad, but remember that you're not dealing with a genuine person in distress. Focus on the solution and stay consistent through the process not allowing your emotions to get the better of you. Leverage your support system during such times and this will help you tide over comfortably. With toxic people removed from your life or new tools in your arsenal to deal with them your life will become better – you will be surrounded by positive people who you enjoy being with and who add value to you as a person.

- Don't compare yourself with others

" From the very beginning you are being told to compare yourself with others. This is the greatest disease; it is like a cancer that goes on destroying your very soul because each individual is unique, and comparison is not possible" – Osho

We live in a world where comparisons are the norm – it starts when you are born – mothers compare height, weight and the overall health score of babies. It goes on with the first word spoken, the first footstep, the first swim, the first tooth sighting and the list goes on. In school parents compare grades, performance in sports, public speaking etc. As you grow the criteria for comparing you also increases – from height and weight when you were born to education, grades, salary, race, class, gender, nationality, the car you drive, the size of your house, your bank balance – the list becomes endless.

I have an interesting small story to narrate here: there was once a very poor man who lived with his wife and 2 kids in a small-dilapidated hut near the King's palace. Every night after an inadequate meal, he would look out from the window towards the palace and imagine the grandeur of the King's life. Accepting his fate he would start to play the violin to his family who would then sleep peacefully. The King inside the palace would look out from his royal mansion after dinner and see this poor family so happily playing the violin and enjoying dinner together. The King says to himself, nobody realizes how tough it is to be in my position – I carry the weight of the entire kingdom on my shoulders, I have to ensure everybody's security, I have to ensure we have enough food to feed our people, taxes get paid. I don't get enough time with my family – we barely manage to see each other – the queen is busy with her appointments. Looking at the poor man in the hut the King says to himself – this man is poor but he is so happy and content – he is living a life devoid of any pressure and stress – he truly is King!

Grass is always greener on the other side – but it doesn't stop us from looking over the fence and feeling sorry for ourselves.

There is, however, a way of making comparisons reasonable and actionable. A reasonable comparison has to be within well-defined parameters e.g. you comparing how well

you play baseball with a teammate. By making this comparison you eliminate obvious differences of age, ability at the sport since you are part of the same team that has a certain standing in the league and make the comparison very specific in nature. On the other hand, if you compare the car you drive with your teammates' then it is an irrational comparison. Compare reasonably and then take action to improve performance on that parameter – continuing with our baseball example – compare your running speed with your teammate and if you are slower then put together a plan to get faster.

In conclusion, don't compare apples with oranges, be happy to see others progress and be satisfied with the path that you are progressing on.

Happiness Index – Measuring how happy you are

"I have been struck again and again by how important measurement is to improving the human condition." - Bill Gates

We have discussed various aspects of happiness so far in this book. What we haven't yet touched upon is how do we measure something as subjective as happiness. How do we quantify it and how do we create a mechanism where we can keep tracking it as time passes by. Mankind has created thorough measurement systems for a multitude of health related metrics like body weight, blood pressure, sugar levels etc. We are fascinated with putting a number to everything around us – but there is no widely available, easy to understand system of measuring and tracking happiness that caters to the broader population. We have said earlier that happiness means different things to different people then how can a single system exist which works for everyone. It can only work if it accommodates the specific needs of every individual using the system.

Id like to briefly touch upon some ways of measuring Happiness developed over the years:

- Satisfaction with life scale (SWLS) developed by psychologist Ed Deiner: The SWLS is a short 5-item instrument designed to measure global cognitive judgments of satisfaction with one's life. The scale usually requires only about one minute of a respondent's time. Participants indicate how much they agree or disagree with each of the 5 items using a 7-point scale that ranges from 7 strongly agree to 1 strongly disagree. The 5-item scale looks as follows:

7 - Strongly agree
6 - Agree
5 - Slightly agree
4 - Neither agree nor disagree
3 - Slightly disagree
2 - Disagree
1 - Strongly disagree

_____ In most ways my life is close to my ideal.
_____ The conditions of my life are excellent.
_____ I am satisfied with my life.
_____ So far I have gotten the important things I want in life.
_____ If I could live my life over, I would change almost nothing.

Though scoring should be kept continuous (sum up scores on each item), here are some cut-offs to be used as benchmarks.

31 - 35 Extremely satisfied
26- 30 Satisfied
21- 25 Slightly satisfied
20   Neutral
15- 19 Slightly dissatisfied
10- 14 Dissatisfied
 5 - 9 Extremely dissatisfied

- Positive and Negative Affect Schedule (PANAS) by Dr. David Watson and Dr. Lee Anna Clark: The Positive and Negative Affect Schedule (PANAS) comprises two mood scales, one that measures positive affect and the other which measures negative affect. Used as a psychometric scale, the PANAS can show relations between positive and negative affect with personality stats and traits. Ten descriptors are used for each PA scale and NA to define their meanings. Participants in the PANAS are required to respond to a 20-item test using 5-point scale that ranges from very slightly or not at all (1) to extremely (5). Reliability and Validity reported by Watson (1988) was moderately good. For the Positive Affect Scale, the Cronbach alpha coefficient was 0.86 to 0.90; for the Negative Affect Scale, 0.84 to 0.87. Over a 8-week time period, the test-retest correlations were 0.47-0.68 for the PA and 0.39-0.71 for the NA. The PANAS has strong reported validity with such measures as general distress and dysfunction, depression, and state anxiety.

- OECD Framework for measuring well-being and progress: In recent years, concerns have emerged regarding the fact that macro-economic statistics, such as GDP, don't provide a sufficiently detailed picture of the living conditions that ordinary people experience. While these concerns were already evident during the years of strong growth and good economic performance that characterised the early part of the decade, the financial and economic crisis has further amplified them. Addressing these perceptions is of crucial importance for the credibility and accountability of public policies but also for the very functioning of democracy. Societal progress is about improvements in the well-being of people and households. Assessing such progress requires looking not only at the functioning of the economic system but also at the diverse experiences and living conditions of people. The OECD Framework for Measuring Well-Being and Progress shown below is based on the recommendations made in 2009 by the Commission on the Measurement of Economic Performance and Social Progress to which the OECD contributed significantly. It also reflects earlier OECD work and various national initiatives in the field. This Framework is built around three distinct domains: material conditions, quality of life and sustainability, each with their relevant dimensions.

- Skills-Based Happiness Quiz by Pursuit-of-happiness.org: The Skills-Based Happiness Quiz measures your "happiness skills" or habits. This Skills-Based Happiness Quiz is based on thousands of scientific studies. Pursuit-of-Happiness.org is a nonprofit organization. Our mission is to support your well-being and the scientific work behind that support. We call this the "Skills-based Happiness Quiz," instead of a depression or anxiety test, because you cantake it to measure concrete life skills related to your happiness, and especially to learn how you can become happier. This quiz, which is based on hundreds of recent scientific studies, focuses on lifestyles and habits that strongly relate to long-term happiness or Psychological Well-Being. In this quiz 13 questions are asked and you respond with how frequently do you exhibit these behaviours.

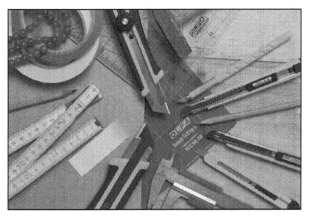

These 13 things have been comprehensively covered in this book – these are activities that are scientifically proven to improve your happiness. The quiz measures your happiness score out of a total of 115 points – the score is essentially a sum of how frequently you exhibit these 13 happiness boosting behaviours or habits. I have found this to be quite useful except the fact that some of these activities may lead to varying degree of happiness among different people. Not everyone values each activity equally and hence the happiness it brings varies. Further, there are times when doing these 13 activities becomes difficult for example when you are hospitalized or when you are going through a rough separation with your partner. During these extreme situations it will be very difficult to pursue these activities. I also think that there can be very few people who can pursue all 13 activities on a daily basis – it doesn't mean that they are not happy. Anyhow, like I said earlier, this is a good metric but has its limitations

Happiness index

"The heart of science is measurement." - Erik Brynjolfsson

In my pursuit of finding a simple model that works for everyone I studied thousands of pages of research and finally came up with a simple weighted average model. This model takes into account your individual preferences – a higher score on the happiness drivers that you value will enhance your overall happiness score more than a lower score on the drivers that you don't care about. I also wanted to ensure that this model is something that everyone should be able to use – it shouldn't need support from a professional psychologist or statistician because quite frankly very few people will ever go to a professional for this model. For that reason, this works for everyone with a basic knowledge of multiplication and addition.

Let us build the model together by first recapping important drivers of happiness:
1. Health
2. Relationships
3. Career/Profession
4. Wealth
5. Sex
6. Hobbies/Recreation
7. Spirituality
8. Others

Now let us put a weight to each of these drivers – choose 0, 1 or 2. 0 when this driver is not important to you at all, 1 when it is important and 2 when it is doubly important to you. This will help you identify the core drivers for your happiness

Let us now apply a scale to the model from 0 to 10 – 0 being extremely dissatisfied and 10 being very satisfied. Ask yourself the question how satisfied am I with my current state of health and put that score in the table below

Weighted score is the result of multiplying the score with the weight

Max score is the maximum score you can get for any driver – it is equal to 10 multiplied by Weight

Now let us try and construct a table with sample data

Driver	Weight (0 – Not important 1- Moderately important 2- Very important)	Score (0 – Extremely dissatisfied 10 – Very satisfied)	Weighted score (Weight multiplied by Score)	Max score (Weight multiplied by 10)
Health	2	8	16	20
Relationships	2	6	12	20
Career/Profession	2	7	14	20
Wealth	2	5	10	20
Sex	2	8	16	20
Hobbies/Recreation	1	6	6	10
Spirituality	1	7	7	10
Others	0	8	0	0
		Grand total	79	120

Your happiness score equals Total of the weighted score divided by Total Max score as a percentage i.e. 79 divided by 120 multiplied by 100; this equals 65.8%

Therefore, the Happiness score for the example above is 65.8%. Let us also look at the detailed score graphically below

Looking at the score graphically shows which areas are relatively important and where the score is not satisfactory. In the example above, it can be clearly seen that Sex, Wealth, Career, Relationships and Health are important drivers for the person; the person is satisfied with Sex, Health and Career but the score on Wealth is not high. So, this person has an area in life that needs some work which is wealth.

Let us take another example

Driver	Weight (0 – Not important 1- Moderately important 2- Very important)	Score (0 – Extremely dissatisfied 10 – Very satisfied)	Weighted score (Weight multiplied by Score)	Max score (Weight multiplied by 10)
Health	1	8	8	10
Relationships	2	1	2	20
Career/Profession	1	10	10	10
Wealth	2	2	4	20
Sex	0	10	0	0
Hobbies/Recreation	2	8	16	20
Spirituality	0	9	0	0
Others	0	8	0	0
		Grand total	40	80

The happiness score of this person is 50% and the graphical depiction is as follows

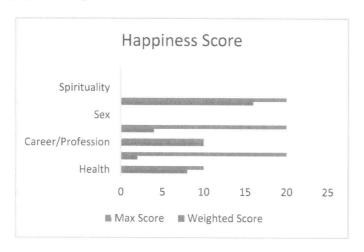

As can be seen, the individual values Hobbies, Wealth and Relationships the most. Unfortunately, his/her score is very low with regard to Wealth and Relationships. The areas of Sex, Spirituality and Others are irrelevant since the individual has given them a zero weight. Despite him/her scoring high scores for Sex and Spirituality at 10 and 9 respectively, it does not add material happiness to the individual's life since he/she has weighted them at zero. This shows a stark imbalance in the individual's life where he/she is doing well in the areas which don't make him happy, and is dissatisfied with the relevant drivers of happiness for him/her.

I encourage you to print out your Happiness Index graph, hold it in your hands and keep it handy when you contemplate about the state of your happiness or life in general. The reason I ask you to do this is that we see and think differently with our hands than with our eyes and heads. Whenever we make something tangible it has the potential to change our perspective. I want your Happiness Index to be the tangible life guide that is always by your side – every time you think about your life you should have it readily available.

There is also a very important use of the graphical depiction of Happiness drivers – it allows you to be able to isolate your problem area. Many times we allow the dissatisfaction with one happiness driver bring down our entire happiness in life. A tiff with your manager, a relationship gone wrong or a bout of illness may lead you to feel dissatisfied with life in general. Our mind tends to follow the communicating vessels logic. Communicating vessels is a system of containers filled with a homogeneous fluid, connected at the base and subjected to the same atmospheric pressure. When the liquid settles, it balances out to the same level in all of the containers regardless of their shape and volume. If additional liquid is added to one vessel, a new equal level will be established in all the connected vessels. This process is part of Stevin's Law and occurs because gravity and pressure are constant in each vessel. Our mind when following the 'Communicating vessels' logic will tend to assume the lowest score for any happiness driver as the overall Happiness score. This is exactly what I want to avoid.

Nevertheless, this graph will help you identify the other happiness drivers which are fine and that in turn should help you put things in perspective. This is a depiction that there is a problem in only one area and not in your entire life. This will help you control your natural instinct to feel dissatisfied with everything in life. Scientists call it 'behavioral spillovers'. No behavior sits in a vacuum, and one behavior can greatly affect what happens next. Behaviors take place sequentially and are linked, at a conscious or unconscious level, by some underlying motive. The first behavior leads to another behavior which can either work in the same direction as the first (promoting spillover), or push back against it (permitting or purging spillover).

		Behavior 2	
		Eat healthy	Eat Less Healthy
Behavior 1	A run after work	**Promoting**	**Permitting**
		I ran an hour, let's keep up the good work	*I ran an hour, I deserve a big slice of cake*
	Sofa-sitting after work	**Purging**	**Promoting**
		I've been lazy today, best not eat so much tonight	*I've been lazy today, so what the heck, let's have a big slice of cake*

I want the Happiness index graphical depiction to act as a promoting force for positive behavioral ripple – every time your mind wanders towards a negative ripple behavior id encourage you to keep the Happiness index infront of your eyes and give it a hard thorough look. It will help you choose the right option and drive you to take action.

I would recommend you to seek professional guidance to sort out specific issues that this tool may highlight. To be able to solve a problem it is important to first acknowledge it – to accept that there is an issue. Often in life we have an issue but we do not acknowledge it, always avoiding looking the issue in the eye and confronting it. It is human tendency to take the easier way out and avoid major upheavel; it is how we are programmed. But by sweeping the issue under the carpet it does not get resolved, to resolve an issue we have to first acknowledge it and then work towards solving it. your happiness index will show you the areas where you need help – but the next step is yours to take – accept that you have an issue and seek professional help. Unfortunately, many people avoid seeking help thinking it makes them look weaker or even feeling ashamed of their situation. This can have negative consequences – knowing you have an issue and not doing something to solve it will only make it worse and the unsolved issue will keep hounding you at all times. By not taking action you allow a bad condition to become worse – an untreated issue can impact other happiness drivers of your life well beyond the problem area.

We have discussed earlier in the book that our life is a journey – much like a flowing river – and our happiness levels do not stay the same. In addition, what makes us happy changes with life, for example when people have kids, kids' happiness becomes an important driver of one's own happiness. So how does this Happiness index help you keep a log of the changing drivers of happiness and your changing happiness scores as you traverse the various twists and turns life throws at you?

To be able to make this tool sustainable we will add a timescale to it – much like a weight chart but with added frills. We will develop some variants together and you can then choose which one you would like to adopt:

- Simple happiness timeline – This can be the most basic variant where you track the overall percentage score over a chosen span of time. Let us start with a monthly tracker

2019	January	February	March	April	May	June	July	August	September	October	November	December
HappIndex	50	65	60	55	65	70	75	80	70	65	60	70

A graphical depiction of the above would look like this

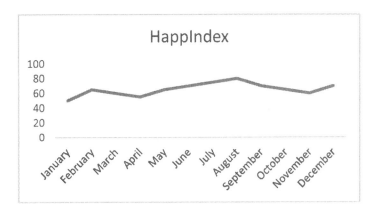

We can elongate the timeline to include multiple years – lets take a 5 year timeline with quarterly scores

Years	Quarter	HappIndex
	Q1	55
	Q2	60
	Q3	75
2019	Q4	70
	Q1	60
	Q2	90
	Q3	65
2020	Q4	60
	Q1	85
	Q2	70
	Q3	65
2021	Q4	50
	Q1	65
	Q2	55
	Q3	75
2022	Q4	70
	Q1	30
	Q2	40
	Q3	50
2023	Q4	65

The corresponding graph would look like this

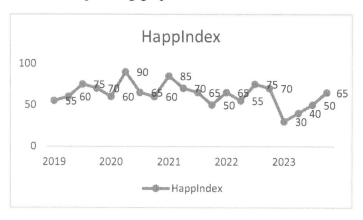

We can extend this over a longer period of time – let's say 10 years and see how it would look like. A decade is a significant duration of our life and can provide valuable insights looking at the decade gone by on what made us happy and what made us sad. It can be a valuable guide for the future – a decade where we can learn from our experiences and avoid committing the same mistakes.

Years	Half	HappIndex
2019	H1	55
	H2	60
2020	H1	75
	H2	70
2021	H1	60
	H2	90
2022	H1	65
	H2	60
2023	H1	85
	H2	70
2024	H1	65
	H2	50
2025	H1	65
	H2	55
2026	H1	75
	H2	70
2027	H1	30
	H2	40
2028	H1	50
	H2	65

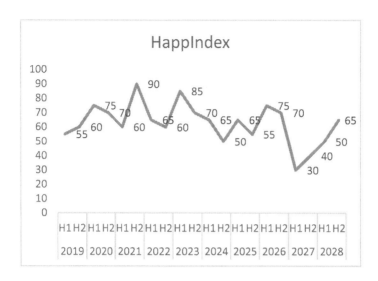

While the above mechanisms give an overview of the score along a timeline, it does not necessarily record what the key drivers of the HappIndex were. If we extend the depiction to include key drivers of happiness and distress, it will become more informative and comprehensive.

- Detailed happiness timeline: In this format, we will also mention key happiness drivers for the Happiness Index in that period.

Years	Quarter	HappIndex	Enhancers	Depletors
	Q1	55	Health, Relationships	Career
	Q2	60	Wealth, Sex	Career
	Q3	75	Relationships, Spirituality	Career
2019	Q4	70	Career, Sex	Relationships
	Q1	60	Career, Spirituality	Relationships, Hobbies
	Q2	90	Wealth, Sex	Relationships
	Q3	65	Spirituality, Wealth	Sex, hobbies
2020	Q4	60	Wealth, Sex	Career
	Q1	85	Relationships, Spirituality	Career
	Q2	70	Career, Sex	Relationships
	Q3	65	Health, Relationships	Career
2021	Q4	50	Wealth, Sex	Career
	Q1	65	Relationships, Spirituality	Career
	Q2	55	Relationships, Spirituality	Career
	Q3	75	Career, Sex	Relationships
2022	Q4	70	Health, Relationships	Career
	Q1	30	Career, Sex	Relationships
	Q2	40	Career, Spirituality	Relationships, Hobbies
	Q3	50	Wealth, Sex	Relationships
2023	Q4	65	Wealth, Sex	Career

'Enhancers' are core drivers of happiness that increase your score – drivers that you weigh heavily and score well on. 'Depletors' are drivers which you weigh heavily but score poorly on. They deplete your overall score and are causing you grief and dissatisfaction. As you look back at your scores and the reasons for that, you will be compelled to think about the 'depletors' in more detail. Often the benefit of hindsight allows us to identify the backstory and separate the truth from fallacies.

Hopefully, this rational analysis of the past incident will provide you with the answers you were searching – what did you do wrong? What did the other person do wrong? Were the circumstances not in your favor? Was the timing off? Were you expecting too much from someone? Did someone exhibit behavior contrary to his or her normal behavior? As they say, what doesn't kill you makes you stronger – every incident or situation in life that you have faced will only equip you to face the next one better.

Living a happy life

Throughout this book I've shared how different cultures, countries and religions profess the practice of happiness and how the principles of ancient wisdom have proven their efficacy through the lens of modern science. I would now like to focus on what you can do on a daily basis to be sustainably happy.

1. Health

    Tip 1: Move your body and control your mind

    Try and get some physical exercise everyday – something that you enjoy doing and something that gets you to sweat and breathe heavily. You don't have to sign up and go to a gym – it can be as simple as brisk walking or climbing stairs or cycling or regularly playing some sport. This also has to be a part of your lifestyle and you should not need to make a huge effort to be able to do this every day. If you go to office every day, try parking at the farthest position from the entrance and walk across the garage twice daily or get down a stop earlier than your stop in the tram or bus and walk the extra mile or shorten your lunch hour and go out for a walk/jog with work buddies. If you are a student, pick up a game which you can play with your friends between classes or in your free time. If you do not want to leave the confines of your home then find an online fitness course and work out at home. If your motion is restricted due to old age or illness then try doing household chores like cleaning the windows, doing the dishes – anything that makes you exert a little.

Controlling the mind is crucial to be able to maintain a balanced view of the situation or the impulse. As soon as your mind starts to take you to extreme thoughts – try to think about something else, something positive which will distract you from the current situation or provide you with much needed reassurance. One practice that works for me is to 'hand over' a problem that I have little control over to my guiding angel. I write down my problem on a piece of paper and physically place it in the spiritual corner in my house – this way I tell my mind that this problem has been handed over to God and that he will take care of it. You can place the piece of paper in front of your guiding angel, in a place of worship, spiritual guru or whoever you believe has special powers and can solve the issue. This may not solve the problem itself, neither can you, but it takes the problem off your mind and frees up space to think about other things. It also doesn't imply that you stop doing efforts to remedy the situation. Focus on remedying the situation rather than stressing about the situation and further fueling anxiety, negativity and inaction.

We all get upset over things that in hindsight do not really matter after 3 months – these sporadic incidences have an adverse impact on not just your own wellbeing but also that of the people around you. Every time something upsets you , think about all the things in your life that are fine. Ask yourself – is this something that I will worry about in 3 months? This way you will be able to control the downward spiral of negative emotions and refocus your mind on positive things.

Tip 2: Eat healthy, sleep well

Food is the fuel for our body and mind – in fact, our brain consumes as much as 20% of all the energy to keep our vital functions running. The quantity and quality of food we eat directly affects our physical and mental ability. The food we eat has evolved a lot over the years; we lived off the land in the stone age but now almost everything can be bought in a can or frozen. There are hundreds of ready-to-eat meals that can be unpacked from a carton/plastic box, 'microwaved' and eaten. This evolution has been necessary as people have less time to cook fresh meals and to feed an ever increasing population food needs to be preserved. Nevertheless, is this healthy for us? According to Medical News Today, processed foods are bad for your health because they contain high amounts of added sugar, artificial (read chemical) ingredients – preservatives, colorants, flavoring, texturants to name a few, refined carbohydrates, have low fiber content and do not have the natural essential nutrients as compared to whole unprocessed foods. Multiple studies show processed foods lead to increased chances of cancer, obesity, high blood pressure, diabetes, heart disease.

I have one simple tip – try to eat like your grandparents did. Across our planet local cuisines have evolved over centuries and have been customized according to what grows in the region, how the climate is, what needs people of the region have and seasonal climatic changes. Thousands of years of wisdom should be valued – it has stood the test of time. Try and have fresh seasonal produce in balanced portion sizes. Replace fizzy drinks and coffee with water – do it gradually and feel the difference to your body and mind.

Just as eating healthy and working out is important – so is sleeping well. Sleep enables the body and the mind to relax, repairs and rejuvenates tissues and muscles, energy is restored and vital hormones are released. Sleep deprivation is associated with heart disease, increased blood pressure, obesity, diabetes and high cholesterol. Researchers at Warwick University and Federico II University Medical school studied analyzed 16 studies involving 1.3 million people and concluded that people should sleep between 6 and 8 hours a day. People sleeping less than 6 hours/day are 12% more likely to die prematurely, excessive sleeping is also not healthy – people sleeping for more than 9 hours a day are 30% more likely to die early.

Many people also have trouble going to sleep – often tumbling and turning in their beds for hours before they doze off.

I have a simple tip to enable you to sleep quickly and peacefully: eat light atleast 2 hours before going to sleep and stop looking at your phone 30 minutes before going to bed. This way you will get high quality uninterrupted sleep and you will wake up refreshed and ready for a bigger challenge everyday

Tip 3: Tell yourself "I've got this" everyday!

"Whatever we plant in our subconscious mind and nourish with repetition and emotion will one day become a reality"—Earl Nightingale

How can you win unless you believe you will win. If your subconscious mind always gets pictures of you losing, how do you think you will perform extraordinarily to win.

Self talk is a form of neuro linguistic programming. It has the potential to mould and sculpt our consciousness because our minds are malleable. Neuro linguistic programming acknowledges the fundamental connection between the brain (neuro), language (linguistic), and our internal and external behaviors (programming). At its core, neuro linguistic programming is a school of thought — but put into practical means, it can be translated as different exercises designed to boost self-awareness, self-esteem, social interactions, and communication skills. Positive self-talk is proven to enhance performance in sportspersons, senior executives in companies and in salespeople closing deals.

Give yourself positive reinforcement before any major event where you are expected to perform – major client presentation, proposing to your girlfriend, asking for a raise, big sports match, live stage performance – the list is endless. When your mind hears "I've got this" – it believes it, confidence increases, self-doubt vanishes, self-image improves and your body gets the necessary rush of hormones needed for high performance.

So make "I've got this" your daily mantra for success

2. Relationships

Tip 4: Two real friends are better than a thousand social media connections

Many of you have relocated for work, studies, love, and marriage often across continents. This has created a geographical barrier to be able to meet your friends regularly for friendly 'banter'. Many times when people move constantly they lose touch with old connections and make new ones. As we age the chances of building new, truly meaningful friendships reduce and we increasingly get caught up with the daily busyness of our routines. Stress in our lives increases and we do not have anyone to share it with; on the contrary, to keep up with social pretenses we end up doing things that add to our stress levels.

To break this negative cycle, what we all need is a 'release valve' – a friend or a group of friends with whom you feel absolutely safe, secure and do not have to worry about the person using the information you disclose to him/her and causing harm. Use technology to stay in touch with real friends even if distances have set you apart. In the famous novel "Top 5 regrets of the dying", palliative nurse Bronnie Ware mentions "I wish I stayed in touch with friends" as the 4th biggest regret. Pick up your phone and speak to your friends now!

Sometimes, there are topics that you are hesitant to share even with the best of your buddies when you are together. These topics may be so personal that you do not wish to disclose them to anyone, like divorce, cheating by your spouse, sexual issues etc Bottling up these negative thoughts and not sharing them with your best friends despite meeting them only adds guilt to the existing stress, worsening the situation. Break this inhibition and speak openly with your trusted friend – you trust them for a reason – have faith in them and speak your heart out. I recommend doing some light exercise/sport together – the adrenaline gives you positive reinforcement and enhanced risk taking ability to be able to share your feelings.

To summarize, leverage your best friends in times of need and share all problems with them. And return the favour when its your turn – true friendship is a two-way street.

Tip 5: Tell the people you love that you love them

The people who are closest to us and support us through everything in life for the longest durations often tend to be taken for granted. When was the last time you explicitly expressed your love to your parents, spouse, brothers, sisters, kids or friends?

In a study conducted by the University of North Carolina, participants were asked to thank their significant other for something, and their interaction was videotaped. The person who was being thanked then rated whether or not their partner had been responsive to them (for example, by showing that they understood and/or liked them). It turned out that people who felt that their significant other had been responsive when thanking them rated their relationship as being higher quality. So if your friend goes out of their way to do something nice for you, don't just say a quick "thanks." Let them know how much their actions mean to you and that you value what they did. In other words, it's not just a polite "thank you," but more about showing the person that you're thinking about them and you care for them.

Its simple to do – but we don't do it – start today and convey your heartfelt gratitude to the people that matter to you the most.

Tip 6: Neutralize toxic people

Toxic people have the uncanny ability to throw you off your pivot position – they will do or say something which imbalances your mental equilibrium and sucks you into a toxic and wasteful situation which can yield nothing positive. How do you know identify these people and how do you manage them? I researched a lot and found the following indicative signs of you being surrounded by toxic people:

- o Their drama emotionally affects you
- o You are not comfortable being around them (read dread)
- o You are stuck in a cycle of helping them fix their problems
- o You are coerced/forced to act in ways that violates your personal values
- o You always have the feeling 'something doesn't smell right'

Anybody you know can be toxic – members of the family, friends, neighbors, coworkers, managers – you cannot control the balance of power in that relationship but you can surely control how you respond to the person. I call this neutralizing toxicity – responding in a way that strengthens your own belief system, taking back control of the situation and freeing yourself from this non-virtuous cycle of negativity.

How do you do that? Start with building courage – tell yourself "I've got this". Then communicate openly and directly – tell the person what is not right and what it is that you will not accept anymore. Be clear, give examples and for a change do not worry about offending the person. Set clear boundaries and maintain consistency in your response to the person. If the person's toxic behavior doesn't change, it's time to cut them loose. Let go of the negativity and drama and focus on positivity all around. Be aware of the cost you will have to bear for taking this decision, specially if the person has significant positional power over you like a boss/manager. Remember the choice is yours – live with a boss who stomps on your self-respect or work in an environment that is more conducive for your personality and self-image.

3. Career/Profession

Tip 7: Take up a profession that you are passionate about and are good at

For many of us career choices have been made based on what the most lucrative career option is at the time – investment banking, computer science, medical studies, professional sportsperson etc There is often lack of knowledge and guidance about the various options available – a choice is made and we stick to it for our entire lives. There are 2 problems with this approach – 1. Business models are getting disrupted at a faster pace than ever before; what could be a hot skill a decade ago may no longer be needed and 2. There is no cognizance of your own ability and passion. All of us are good at some things and terrible at others – we like some things and don't like some others – this gives us a higher probability of success in some areas.

We have spoken about the concept of Ikigai earlier in the book – I find it to be hugely rational – do what you love and what you are good at. There is no point in doing what you do not like – you will never be able to bring your best ability to it and consequently will never succeed. Equally important is to be good at what you do; even if you love playing baseball more than anything else in life but cannot swing a bat well then do not take it up. You will never be able to climb up the ladder of success and win.

For a lot of us, we have spent a significant portion of our lives in our current professional and it would not be possible to completely walk away from it without significant impact on our financial status and the resulting impact on our family. For such instances, I would recommend pursuing your passion as hobbies – art, social service, caring for the elderly, sports – pour your energy into what you truly love during your non-work hours. The resulting increase in happiness will boost your motivation at work and propel you to perfection and eventually success.

For others, who are willing to ride through a bigger change there are ways to try out what you love. There are many success stories of how people have changed careers later on in their life and catapulted to unprecedented success. Harrison Ford, before he became Indiana Jones was a professional carpenter for 15 years. The famous talk show host Ellen Degeneres had a string of jobs before she made a name for herself in comedy and eventually succeeded as a talk show host. There are numerous such examples – but before you take the plunge prepare yourself for the consequences of your decisions and that success is not guaranteed. Not everyone who takes the plunge becomes successful.

Tip 8: Never work long hours – except for a real emergency

There is a myth that people who work harder (quantified by the measure of hours you dedicate to your job) are more successful. In a lot of business literature the words 'smart', 'hardworking' and 'successful' are used in the same sentence. They have almost become synonyms – people who work hard are smart people and successful people.

I strongly disagree with this notion – and so does research. In a study of consultants by Erin Reid, a professor at Boston University's Questrom School of Business, managers could not tell the difference between employees who actually worked 80 hours a week and those who just pretended to. While managers did penalize employees who were transparent about working less, Reid was not able to find any evidence that those employees actually accomplished less, or any sign that the overworking employees accomplished more.

Research from the Stanford University have revealed that the output among employees falls crucially after they work for 50 hours in a week and further it falls rapidly after 55 hours in a week. Someone who works for 70 hours or more doesn't produce anything more than the extra 15 hours. Long hours have been connected with employee turnover and absenteeism.

Pew Research reveals that 38% of adults claim that email, internet and smartphones have definitely increased the total amount of working hours. In case of those who work at offices, the number soars up to 48%.

It is even a bigger concern that employees are compromising their sleep for work. The Pennsylvania University researchers examined the studies and eventually found out the critical fact that people who claimed that they slept 6 hours (or even less than that) at night, worked 2 hours more than the average time as against those who slept for more hours. We have discussed earlier how important sleep is for all of us.

The research is loud and clear - overworking beyond a limit does not produce any additional benefits to your employer and is detrimental to your health.

I would recommend 2 things – 1. Don't work more than 40 hours in a normal week (50 if there is a 'really' important project) and 2. Try and sync your work rhythm with your body clock.

How would you go about changing the status quo? Start by having a dialogue with your manager – try to shift your mutual focus on the deliverables for the job and not the time spent in office. If you become totally focused on deliverables then it will stop mattering to both of you when you come to the office and when you leave. If your work timings are flexible, try to adapt your work cycle to your body clock – if you are a morning person then start working earlier and leave earlier. If you are a night owl then start late and work till late. If your commute to the office is long and cumbersome – ask for the occasional home office day; try to avoid rush hour traffic and save yourself additional stress, earn brownie points for contributing positively to the planet and save fuel expenses too.

Making these small adjustments will hugely enhance your productivity, reduce stress and free up time.

4. Wealth

Tip 9: Build wealth – so you can enjoy life

Some of life's joys don't cost a dime but many do and much more than a dime. Your ability to exercise your wishes and that of your family is directly dependent on your financial situation. You either have the money for it or not. I'm not talking about austerity lessons that we would like to give our kids to teach them the value of money – when we have the money to buy what they want but we delay the purchase or buy a cheaper version of the product to keep their expectations in check. I'm talking about the simple concept of financial strength. Do you have the financial ability to fulfil the reasonable demands of your family or not? If your answer is 'no' – then this is a clear area to take action on. Before I get into how I think you can improve your financial situation – I'd like to elaborate on the term I used earlier 'reasonable demands'. This is a subjective term and the definition of reasonable will vary from person to person. What is a reasonable holiday to you may be an extravagant holiday for someone else and vice versa – I will not go into this further but you get the drift.

The fundamental point here is that a reasonably good life costs money – if you do not have enough to live a reasonably good life there will be a constant dampener to your happiness. So how do we fix this?

I recommend a 3-point financial agenda

- Disciplined approach to finances: Track what you spend your money on – assess whether you need all that, reduce unnecessary/avoidable expenditures, create an expense plan and diligently stick to it. Budget for unexpected events and create a small emergency fund for such situations.

- Creating additional sources of income: Most people in the world have a single source of income but all the rich people become rich by creating additional sources of income. In today's world where gig opportunities are abundant and technology has reduced traditional barriers I strongly believe that if you want to earn more money you can. Try to commercialize your passion – Are you a great gardener? Can you help your neighbors design and maintain their garden? If you are an artist, can you not try to sell your art on the plethora of platforms available today? Can you not drive for Uber/Lyft and earn an extra buck sometimes? Can you not give after school tuitions to school graders? Can you rent out your garage? Where there is a will there is a way – start small but start now – remember no work is lowly and you are doing this to bring a smile to your family's face and secure your and their future.

- Investment: Let your money work for you! It is not surprising that all the financial jargon thrown at them by finance gurus scares many people. Combine this with the lack of knowledge on how and where to invest and the perception that investing is for rich people only, keeps millions of people away from participating in financial markets. This is a massive lost opportunity. There are specialized apps (like Stash, Digit, Qapital etc) which allow people to invest even small amounts safely and with full transparency.

Don't wait any longer, take charge of your finances and take charge of life

'You must gain control over your money or the lack of it will forever control you.'
-Dave Ramsey
Tip 10: Money is not everything
'A wise person should have money in their head, but not in their heart.'
-Jonathan Swift

We all agree that money is important – but it has its own place in life. Blindly chasing more and more of it in life will only lead to more greed and more desire. Benjamin Franklin once said, 'Money never made a man happy yet, nor will it. The more a man has, the more he wants. Instead of filling a vacuum, it makes one.' When you have a million, you look at the person who has ten, when you have ten you look at the person who has hundred and so on – this is an endless cycle. Always remember that money can only buy things – it cannot buy you true friends, it cannot buy you the love of your kids, it can buy you an expensive bed but cannot buy you sound sleep, it can buy time with the best doctors but cannot buy good health, it can buy expensive food but cannot make you hungry.

Many people are going to extreme lengths to earn money often compromising on aspects that they end up repenting later on. Someone told me about a couple – both Ivy League educated, working in different cities in highflying corporate jobs not having the time to take care of their kids who are living with their grandparents. They justify this lifestyle by saying it creates a secure financial future for their kids. I agree that they are able to provide better 'things' for their kids like clothes, books, toys and gadgets but are they really being good parents? Do the kids not need their parents? Does the provision of things fulfil the child's desire to be with his/her parents? Can this time spent apart be recovered? These are some of the questions I would encourage you to ask yourself when taking decisions about money that affect other aspects of life.

'Money is only a tool. It will take you wherever you wish, but it will not replace you as the driver.'
-Ayn Rand

5. Sex

Tip 11: Make sex a priority

Earlier in the book I spoke about how important sex is to humans – it makes us both healthier and happier almost like a wonder drug with no side effects! Despite the benefits, research suggests we are having less sex than our grandparents did.

According the General Social Survey, a profile of American behavior that has been gathered by the

National Opinion Research Council at the University of Chicago since 1972, the fraction of people having sex at least once a week fell from 45% in 2000 to 36% in 2016. One study of the GSS data showed that more than twice as many millennials were sexually inactive in their early 20s than the prior generation was. And this is despite the social stigma of premarital sex being gone, casual sex becoming increasingly acceptable, increase in homosexual activity and reduced social stigmatization as compared to the past and all the advances in technology which make meeting new mates easier and less awkward. There are other catalysts to increased sexual activity – an almost unlimited supply of porn to rev the engine and marvels of modern medicine that allow men to overcome physical limitations. Despite all these advances, we are having less sex. Why?

Our modern lifestyle is the primary culprit – busy jobs, after work drinks, travel, meetings, social events, kids' time, sports time, buddy time, phone time, TV time, internet time – we make time for everything except sex. It has fallen in our priority list and has become the rare occurrence that happens when nothing else can come in the way and there is still energy left to do it.

That is a dismal picture that must change – but how?

By prioritizing it over everything else – rather than waiting for the kids to sleep after a grueling day and hoping for energy to be left for sex – start your day with it! Wake up and rather than hitting the yoga mat get some action between the sheets first. Be shameless in asking for it and keep trying new things that surprise your partner. Try to sneak in sex in your routine – it does not have to be a scheduled activity in your calendar. It is also not an activity restricted for young people alone, as you age find ways of pleasuring yourself.

Live a sexually active life – and if it is not active at the moment – make it active

6. Hobbies/Recreation

Tip 12: Follow your passion, passionately

Majority of the people in the world choose their careers before they realize what their true passion is or have multiple interest areas that can all not become full time professions or we like to do different things during different phases of our lives. There is always something that you love to do but often cannot find enough time to do it. There is always something else that takes priority – kids, relatives, friends, work – we do everything else except what we love. The result is predictable – a monotonous, uninspiring life which becomes mechanical in nature and devoid of any pleasure/happiness. Without any release valve for stress, it accumulates over time and manifests itself in sickness and disease. What we need is an intermittent pressure release that also rejuvenates us. Hobbies serve exactly that purpose – because we like doing them we get in the flow very quickly, it gives us the escape from the monotony of daily life, and the stress associated with it.

I would highly encourage you to start doing what you like outside of work – it could be gardening, woodwork, reading, playing music, stamp collecting, handicraft, art, bonsai, origami or anything that you have loved doing in your life. Many people I meet say they do not know what their hobby could be – to you people I say start exploring – try new things and maybe you start to like something that you have tried. Be selfish and make time for it – be unapologetic about it and do not let guilt draw you into not taking that time out for yourself. There are certain hobbies that can be done over varying time durations, like Golf – if you don't have time for 18-hole, play 9-hole or go to the driving range and hit 50 balls and reduce your time commitment but still do what you enjoy. Avoid making a binary decision – I do it or I don't do it – find the sweet spot which suits your schedule.

"A hobby a day keeps the doldrums away" – Phyllis McGinley

7. Spirituality

Tip 13: Believe in a superpower watching over you – taking care of you

A few generations ago, families were larger, multiple adults stayed under one roof and split up daily tasks – someone would go get the groceries, someone else would drop the kids to school, someone would take care of the cooking, someone would take care of finances – everybody in the large family contributed to the normal functioning of the household. In the baby-boomer era, families became nuclear – a couple and their kids living under one roof. This brought with it a wider responsibility for people – all tasks of the household needed to be done by the two adults in the family. Modern day life is even more individualistic – we are crumbling under all that we have to do, to just 'keep the lights on'. We all seem to be carrying the weight of the world on our shoulders – and by the time Friday draws to a close we are completely drained and looking forward to the weekend to be able to relax and catch a breath.

If you take a step back and think about it more deeply – you are fighting alone – against the whole world. Just think how horrible it feels – lonely, disempowering, unfair and difficult.

Wouldn't it be fantastic if you had someone who would be helping you along the way – and didn't ask for anything in return? Well, all major religions in the world have given us exactly that – God to believe in who will protect us, guide us and help us achieve our goals. In Judaism linked Rabbinic literature, the Rabbis expressed the notion that there are indeed guardian angels appointed by God to watch over people.

Rashi on Daniel 10:7 "Our Sages of blessed memory said that although a person does not see something of which he is terrified, his guardian angel, who is in heaven, does see it; therefore, he becomes terrified

In Christianity - according to Saint Jerome, the concept of guardian angels is in the "mind of the Church". He stated, "how great the dignity of the soul, since each one has from his birth an angel commissioned to guard it".

In Islamic tradition a guardian angel or lit. Watcher angel (raqib "watcher") is an angel which maintains every being in life, sleep, death or resurrection. These angels are included in the 'hafazhah' ("the guards") and Muhammad is reported to have said that every man has ten guardian angels.

In Hinduism, people pray to a diverse array of Gods who will each do something in return – many offer protection from evil or bad occurrences in one's life. Even today majority of Hindus tie a saffron colored thread around their wrists to 'protect' them from the wrath of the unknown. Many people wear rings to avoid trouble from angry planets, many perform rituals called 'yagnas' to appease Gods and avoid untoward occurrences in their lives.

The concept of the guiding angel therefore reinforces our ability to fight through daily life and have the feeling that some super power is taking care of us.

I would recommend that you believe in some super power watching over you and your loved ones – associate a symbol or a thing like a necklace or an armband or a ring and believe that your guardian angel has your back. You will see yourself becoming comfortable in moments of doubt.

8. Others

Tip 14: Do good for others – specially the needy

When was the last time you did something for someone who cannot pay you back – think how it made you feel. Did you not feel elated at being able to do something that helped a person in need tremendously? Why do you not do it more often? What is stopping you? Are you giving the excuse of not having enough time or money despite spending countless hours on social media and other wasteful expenses?

Think again, the moral code of humanity is that we help one another. Every great tragedy in our history has brought to the fore great stories of humans helping each other. Survival is our most basic instinct and its best comes out during times of distress when people start to help each other, forget their differences and do it for the sake of humanity.

Go out there and start helping others – nothing is small or insignificant - volunteer for a cause, take care of the elderly, help a kid with their homework, offer your seat to the needy in a bus, do anything that brings a smile to someone's face. Even if you do not believe in good karma, you at least get to see one additional smiling face.

"No one is useless in this world who lightens the burdens of another." Charles Dickens

Tip 15: Reduce clutter, chaos and social media distractions

Our lives have become a junkyard of technology, apps, devices and things – how much time did you spend last week on your mobile phone responding to the hundreds or thousands of messages, updates, emails, alerts, news flashes etc? How much time and effort do you spend charging and updating the software of your tens of devices? 20 years ago we weren't surrounded by tech gadgets – travelers had almost no tech products in their bags – today we are all travelling with 2 phones, 1 laptop, 1 tablet, 1 headset, 1 powerbank and all the wires that come with them. There isn't an uglier sight than the sight of jumbled up cables – this is how our lives have become – jumbled up by things that are consuming us more than they should. We have too much of everything – clothes, shoes, belts, cars, caps, furniture, utensils, equipment – we own far more than we need and all this unused stuff weighs in on our minds.

Start throwing things out that you do not need – better still, donate them to the needy. Buy only what you really need – yes the emphasis here is on 'really'. Change the notification settings on your phone so that you look at it only after every 3 hours when you do not need to. Rent the stuff you need less than 5 times a year. Free up space, free up your mind and immerse yourself in other activities that really make you happy.

"Out of clutter, find simplicity." Albert Einstein

The last and most important tip

"Nobody gets everything in life – appreciate what you have"

Pick any great personality, read about their life and you will realize they had their great strengths because of which they became famous and successful, but they also had their weaknesses and shortcomings. They have all had imperfections in their life – some people died early, some lost their loved ones, some could never find true love, or found it so many times that it caused major upheavals, some had psychological problems, substance abuse issues, health issues, involvement in unlawful incidents, social expulsion, imprisonment and torture – nobody, I repeat nobody has had a life without their share of challenges and shortcomings.

Life is not meant to be perfect, it is to be lived, and happiness is what makes it sweet. So,

"Sit back, relax and enjoy the ride called life"

Conclusion

"In theory there is no difference between theory and practice. In practice there is." – Yogi Berra

I spent the last few years of my life researching for and authoring this book. I sincerely hope this would have provided you with some life skills you can practice to be happier and lead more satisfying lives while achieving the goals that you work hard towards. I cannot emphasize how important practice is – all theory is of no use if we don't get up and practice it. So stop thinking, get up and start doing...now!

"Sharing your joy doubles it, sharing your grief halves it." – Indian proverb

If this book has inspired you, helped you in the smallest of ways possible - spread the word – follow me on social media and continue to receive my life changing happiness tips
Twitter: @HAPPY_SODA_1
LinkedIn: https://www.linkedin.com/in/rohit-sodha-80388386/

I also provide personal counselling sessions to people needing help. I do it in a non-traditional way, I don't sit on a sofa taking notes in a room - we do interesting activities together (like Golf, Nordic walking, Squash, Yoga) and while doing these activities we discuss the topics important to my clients.

20% of my time is allocated for people who cannot afford my services, it is my way of giving back to society.

If you would like to book time with me for a personal session please reach out to me via the following various social media channels.
Facebook: rohit.sodha.1
Twitter: @HAPPY_SODA_1
Instagram: rohit_sodha_81

Acknowledgment

What started as a hobby turned into an obsession, this obsession carried me through thousands of hours of research and gave me the courage to pen my first book. As I write this acknowledgement, I realize that my education on the topic of happiness already started when I was a child – I just did not realize it back then. I was fortunate to be surrounded by people who were role models for society, you may not have heard their names but ask the people they helped and they will tell you how these few people changed the lives of thousands of people, one at a time. I learnt the meaning of the word 'giving' very early in my life. To me it is the most empowering and satisfying feeling that there is – to be able to have positive impact on the lives of others.

I'm grateful to a lot of people for their tremendous contributions –

- My parents who always believed in me and supported every decision I took knowing that my life's journey is going to be unique and allowing me to have my own experiences
- My sister for always showing me how to do things better and for being brutally honest and very caring at the same time
- My wife for tolerating me and being the pillar of strength she is for me
- My sons for being a better version of what I could have been as a child and a reflection of my forefathers
- My uncles for being the guardian angels of my life, protecting me and picking me up every time I fall

- My cousins who I look up to for the grace and poise they exhibit while overcoming adversity
- My parents in law for entrusting me with their most prized possession and for expanding my intellectual horizon
- My friends for having supported me through all times and lightening up the grimmest of situations

I would like to express my gratitude to the teachers and staff of St. Pauls High School, Agra where I acquired primary education, teachers and staff of Delhi Pubic School R K Puram where I acquired secondary education. The Dean of my engineering school at Indraprastha University, Mr. Gurmeet Singh Soin who showed me the true meaning of leadership and encouraged me to start on the journey. Inspiring faculty and staff of Fore School of Management and Harvard Business School. My colleagues at McKinsey and Co., DHL, Snapdeal, my startup and Amazon.

Special shout out to my team who made this book possible – Sandeep Singh for graphic design and research support, Kamer Aktas for photographing me and making me look good.

My friends Ping Chen, Eva Jelnikar, Shirley Liu, Cindy Dennis, Yap-Seng Chong for taking time out from their busy schedules and reviewing the content and suggesting improvements.

Sources of information

1. https://en.wikipedia.org/wiki/Happiness
2. https://en.wikipedia.org/wiki/Eudaimonia
3. Philosophyterms.com
4. https://greatergood.berkeley.edu/article/item/six_ways_happiness_is_good_for_your_health
5. Positive affect measured using ecological momentary assessment and survival in older men and women - Andrew Steptoe and Jane Wardle
6. https://www.apa.org/pubs/journals/releases/psp805804.pdf
7. https://www.sciencedirect.com/science/article/pii/S030105110900235X
8. http://www.smf.co.uk/wp-content/uploads/2015/10/Social-Market-Foundation-Publication-Briefing-CAGE-4-Are-happy-workers-more-productive-281015.pdf#page=9
9. https://hbr.org/2011/06/the-happiness-dividend
10. https://www.sciencedaily.com/releases/2011/08/110822091859.htm
11. https://www.cnbc.com/2017/08/09/the-happiest-countries-in-the-world-also-pay-a-lot-in-taxes.html
12. https://www.thebestbrainpossible.com/how-happy-happens-in-your-brain/
13. Lagom – Lola A Akerstrom
14. http://hyggehouse.com/hygge
15. https://www.currentresults.com/Weather/Europe/Cities/sunshine-annual-average.php

16. Ikigai: The Japanese Secret to a Long and Happy Life by Hector Garcia and Francesc Miralles
17. Happinessaroundtheglobe.com
18. *Smith, E. R.; Mackie, D. M. (2007). Social Psychology (Third ed.). Hove: Psychology Press*
19. https://blog.iqmatrix.com/self-image
20. https://paindoctor.com/top-10-stressful-life-events-holmes-rahe-stress-scale/
21. https://www.huffingtonpost.co.uk/2015/01/07/top-ten-happiest-moments-in-life_n_6429144.html
22. https://www.verywellfamily.com/grandparents-and-grandchildren-keeping-them-close-1695871
23. https://www.care.com/c/stories/5762/things-grandchildren-learn-from-grandparents/
24. https://www.independent.co.uk/life-style/science-parents-successful-children-13-things-in-common-list-a7711611.html
25. https://oureverydaylife.com/teenagers-importance-friends-6135.html
26. https://www.theglobeandmail.com/life/why-adolescence-is-the-most-important-part-of-our-lives/article4274456/
27. http://ec.europa.eu/eurostat/statistics-explained/index.php/Duration_of_working_life_-_statistics#Development_over_the_period_2000_-_2016
28. http://smallbusiness.chron.com/behavior-company-managers-can-affect-behaviors-subordinates-23552.html

29. https://www.statista.com/statistics/24569
    4/influence-of-friends-and-family-on-
    american-teenagers-decisions-regarding-
    sex/
30. http://raisingchildren.net.au/articles/peer_
    pressure_teenagers.html
31. http://time.com/4506490/happy-people-
    make-their-spouses-healthier/
32. https://www.webmd.com/healthy-
    aging/features/importance-of-marriage#1
33. http://www.bbc.com/capital/story/201805
    02-how-your-workplace-is-killing-you
34. https://www.stress.org/workplace-stress/
35. https://www.health.harvard.edu/healthbea
    t/the-happiness-health-connection
36. https://en.wikipedia.org/wiki/Mens_sana
    _in_corpore_sano
37. https://www.huffingtonpost.com/anca-
    dumitru/health-tips_b_3792302.html
38. http://www.ewellnessmag.com/article/7-
    steps-to-keeping-your-body-healthy
39. https://www.healthline.com/health/balanc
    ed-diet
40. https://www.rd.com/health/conditions/am
    erica-sleep-crisis/
41. https://www.livestrong.com/article/34970
    2-ways-to-keep-your-body-healthy/
42. http://techtimeout.com/three-ways-
    technology-impacts-sleep/
43. https://www.mentalhealth.gov/basics/wha
    t-is-mental-health
44. https://en.wikipedia.org/wiki/Mental_hea
    lth
45. https://www.uhs.umich.edu/tenthings

46. https://www.helpguide.org/articles/mental-health/building-better-mental-health.htm
47. http://www.thehindu.com/features/education/research/man-as-a-social-animal/article2988145.ece
48. https://www.takingcharge.csh.umn.edu/why-personal-relationships-are-important
49. http://www.nmbreakthroughs.org/wellness/5-benefits-of-healthy-relationships
50. http://www.happy-relationships.com/types-of-relationships.html
51. https://successstory.com/inspiration/why-success-is-important-to-us
52. https://www.huffingtonpost.com/grant-cardone/importance-of-success_b_837924.html
53. https://hbr.org/2013/05/why-men-work-so-many-hours
54. http://www.businessinsider.com/how-money-affects-the-most-important-things-in-life-2015-8?IR=T
55. http://www.psypost.org/2018/02/large-amount-wealth-linked-increased-happiness-especially-among-earned-50767
56. https://www.inc.com/peter-cohan/will-10-million-make-you-happier-harvard-says-yes-if-you-make-it-yourself-give-it-away.html
57. https://www.psychologytoday.com/us/articles/199901/men-women-and-money
58. http://time.com/4809325/friends-friendship-health-family/

59. https://www.bustle.com/articles/113750-
3-problems-people-from-toxic-families-
often-struggle-with
60. https://www.huffingtonpost.com/entry/ho
w-your-sex-life-affects-your-
relationship_us_56c4df41e4b08ffac1276
af5?guccounter=1
61. http://www.chatelaine.com/health/sex-
and-relationships/more-sex-is-the-secret-
to-a-longer-healthier-life/
62. http://psychologytomorrowmagazine.com
/popuartic-alyssa-siegel-my-cheating-
heart/
63. https://www.huffingtonpost.com/michele
-weinerdavis/10-things-you-must-know-
a_b_7247708.html
64. https://www.theatlantic.com/magazine/ar
chive/2017/10/why-happy-people-
cheat/537882/
65. http://www.bbc.com/earth/story/2016021
3-why-pairing-up-for-life-is-hardly-ever-
a-good-idea
66. https://qz.com/984174/silicon-valley-has-
idolized-steve-jobs-for-decades-and-its-
finally-paying-the-price/
67. https://insights.som.yale.edu/insights/are-
ceos-todays-heroes
68. https://hbswk.hbs.edu/item/are-todays-
business-heroes-challenging-our-ideas-
about-leadership
69. https://www.weforum.org/agenda/2018/0
1/the-countries-where-people-work-the-
longest-hours/
70. https://www.weforum.org/agenda/2016/0
9/think-working-long-hours-is-a-good-
thing-this-is-why-you-re-wrong

71. https://www.psychologytoday.com/us/blo
g/happy-trails/201509/six-reasons-get-
hobby
72. https://www.theguardian.com/commentis
free/2016/jan/11/hobbies-happier-
gardening-bird-watching-stroking-cat
73. https://www.happymelly.com/can-
hobbies-make-you-happier/
74. https://www.dermascope.com/wellness/h
ow-hobbies-lead-to-happiness-at-work-
and-in-life
75. http://time.com/4857777/generosity-
happiness-brain/
76. https://www.psychologytoday.com/intl/bl
og/the-mindful-self-express/201511/how-
gratitude-leads-happier-life
77. https://www.bakadesuyo.com/2015/11/ho
w-to-stop-feeling-guilty/
78. http://www.thelawofattraction.com/remo
ving-toxic-people-life/
79. http://labs.psychology.illinois.edu/~edien
er/SWLS.html
80. https://backend.fetzer.org/sites/default/fil
es/images/stories/pdf/selfmeasures/SATI
SFACTION-SatisfactionWithLife.pdf
81. https://www.statisticssolutions.com/positi
ve-and-negative-affect-schedule-panas/
82. DOI:https://doi.org/10.1787/9789264191
655-en
83. http://www.pursuit-of-happiness.org/
84. https://www.sciencedirect.com/science/ar
ticle/pii/S0167487014001068
85. https://www.independent.co.uk/life-
style/health-and-families/features/what-
happens-to-your-body-when-you-sleep-
a6675861.html

86. https://www.telegraph.co.uk/news/health/news/7677812/People-who-sleep-for-less-than-six-hours-die-early.html
87. https://medium.com/change-your-mind/reprogramming-your-subconscious-mind-ecaae9640aad
88. https://www.ncbi.nlm.nih.gov/pubmed/23731434
89. https://hbr.org/2015/08/the-research-is-clear-long-hours-backfire-for-people-and-for-companies
90. http://time.com/5297145/is-sex-dead/

Made in the USA
San Bernardino, CA
05 December 2019